Contents

Acknowledgements iii

About the authors iv

Editorial xi

Section 1: Policy and campaigns 1

Autistic people and Transforming Care: what do we know?
Professor Chris Hatton 3

Challenging the ideology of idealised normalcy
Dr Damian EM Milton 7

Rethinking housing for people with autism and intellectual disability
Dr Mitzi Waltz 11

Safeguarding autistic adults in England
Dr Yo Dunn 15

Section 2: Participatory research methods 23

A socio-legal analysis of the Mental Capacity Act (2005) and its implications for participation in autism-related research
Gillian Loomes 25

Engaging 'seldom-heard' individuals in participatory autism research
Professor Elizabeth Pellicano 29

Refocusing: what you see isn't all there is – getting healthcare right in hospitals for autistic and learning disabled people
Jim Blair, Mary Busk, Simon Hawtrey-Woore, Ismail Kaji, Ciara Lawrence,
Gail Moody, Yvonne Newbold, Lauretta Ofulue 35

Towards meaningful participation in research and support practice: effecting change in autism services
Dr Joseph Long and Alastair Clarkson 41

Knowing me – knowing me: Changing the story around stigma and 'behaviours of concern'; promoting self-awareness, self-control and a positive narrative
Professor Richard Mills and Dr Michael McCreadie 47

Section 3: From theory to practice 51

Considering employment of young people with intellectual impairment and autism leaving school and college
Chris Barnham and Professor Nicola Martin 53

Employment: a reflective review
Dr Damian EM Milton 59

Mental health and autism
Dr Eddie Chaplin 63

Autism, learning disability, and the criminal justice system
Dr Luke Beardon and Dr Libby Gaskell 69

The use of spit hoods by the police on autistic suspects
Kleio Cossburn 75

Accessible information within the criminal justice system
Professor Sarah Parsons 79

Autism, intellectual impairment and old age
Professor Nicola Martin and Joanna Krupa 83

Useful resources from Pavilion 88

Acknowledgements

The editors would like to thank the full editorial and review panel and all the authors that have contributed to this volume. We are also very grateful to Joanna Krupa for her administrative support.

Finally, we would like to thank Pavilion Publishing and the Participatory Autism Research Collective (PARC) for their ongoing support.

This volume is dedicated to the memory of LB (Laughing Boy), Connor Sparrowhawk.

About the authors

Chris Barnham

Chris Barnham is a visiting fellow in the Centre for Educational Research at London South Bank University. He is a policy and strategy consultant and writer, and former senior civil servant with extensive experience in delivering policy and change in education, children's services and employment. His new novel, *Fifty One*, is out soon.

Jim Blair

Jim Blair is currently a consultant nurse intellectual (learning) disabilities at Great Ormond Street Hospital in London, associate professor intellectual (learning) disabilities at Kingston University and St Georges' University of London as well as clinical advisor learning disabilities NHS England. He is also the health advisor at the British Institute of learning disabilities and the learning disability advisor to the sates of Jersey and Guernsey.

From 2008-2013 Jim was consultant nurse learning disabilities at St. George's Hospital in London ensuring safe lawful and timely care was delivered in partnership with people with learning disabilities.

Between 2006 and 2009 Jim was president of the Royal Society of Medicine's council for the Forum on Intellectual Disability. From 2011-2013 Jim was vice chairman of Special Olympics Great Britain. Jim is an expert advisor to the Parliamentary Health Service Ombudsman, an advisor for the Down Syndrome Medical Interest Group and is on the editorial board of www.intellectualdisability.info. Jim is also a specialist clinical advisor to the Care Quality Commission.

Dr Luke Beardon

Luke Beardon has worked in the autism field in a wide range of capacities for over twenty years. From a hands-on practitioner working in residential services through to various roles at The National Autistic Society including head of training and consultancy, Luke is currently senior lecturer in autism at Sheffield Hallam University. He is the course leader for the Post Graduate Certificate in Autism and Asperger Syndrome. He is the recipient of The National Autistic Society's award for an educational professional and an autism hero lifetime achievement award winner, inspirational teacher, and inspirational research supervisor.

Kabie Brook

Kabie Brook is an autistic activist and campaigner, co-founder and current chairperson of ARGH (Autism Rights Group Highland), and has 25 years' experience working with and for autistic people of all ages. Kabie is a member of the National Autism Strategy Governance Group (Scotland), has helped develop training materials for the National Autistic Society (NAS), is a community advisor for Police Scotland and is currently working with Dinah Murray and Kevin Brook on the ASK (Autistic Space Kit app), now available. In 2016 Kabie organised and led the first Autistic Europe Fringe. She is committed to creating useful autistic-led spaces and the promotion of autistic-led initiatives. Kabie is passionate about educating people to understand the communication styles and self-advocacy attempts that can often be ignored or labelled as 'challenging' and believes that it is the autistic community and those who use services who should be given the power to take control and steer what is currently an inadequate system of 'existence' rather than 'living' for far too many people.

Dr Eddie Chaplin

Eddie Chaplin is an associate professor at London South Bank University. He has extensive clinical experience managing and working in a range of local and national mental health services for people with intellectual disabilities and autism. Eddie is editor for the journal *Advances in Autism*, and published the first guided self-help manual specifically aimed at people with intellectual disabilities and autism. His current research is examining neurodevelopmental conditions in the criminal justice system.

Alastair Clarkson

Alastair Clarkson is researcher in residence at Scottish Autism and a PhD candidate in education at the University of Aberdeen. He holds an MSc in autism studies from Strathclyde University and previously worked as an autism practitioner in Scottish Autism's services.

Kleio Cossburn

Kleio Cossburn has personal experience of autism and served as a police officer with the Cheshire police until she was retired due to ill-health. She then completed a HE certificate in theology and went on to study for a Bachelor of Health Science degree. In 2013 Kleio began a postgraduate certificate in autism at Sheffield Hallam University. Dr Luke Beardon, Dr Nick Chown and Dr Damian Milton became her inspiration to continue with her education, offering both support and opportunities as a researcher.

Kleio is a founding member of the 'High Achievers' research team that has investigated the support for autistic students at universities in the UK. She has also acted as a reviewer for autism research, offering feedback to researchers. Her latest review was of the National Autistic Society's *Autism: A guide for police officers and staff*.

Kleio is now studying criminology and linking this to her knowledge and experience of autism and policing. She has been offered a place on a Professional Doctorate where her research theme will continue to be in the field of policing and autism.

Dr Yo Dunn

Yo is an independent trainer and consultant who works across the public sector (primarily in social care and education) with specialisms in autism and in law. She has expertise on the legal framework of adult social care in particular and on a range of areas of public law relevant to the lives of autistic people including the Care Act and adult social care law broadly; safeguarding; legal aspects of commissioning; mental capacity law; deprivation of liberty; special educational needs and disability law; health law; data protection; equality and human rights law. She provides training and consults for many English local authorities and other clients (sometimes on behalf of Belinda Schwehr's Care and Health Law). This includes providing legal updates underpinned by her reporting of new case law in all these areas for care and health law. She has also managed two service improvement projects funded by the Scottish government working closely with schools and across multiple agencies to improve autism knowledge and practice in the mid-Highland area.

Yo regularly speaks at national and international conferences in her fields of expertise. She is currently a member of the Scientific Committee for the Autism Europe Congress to be held in Edinburgh in September 2016 and of the expert and autistic advisory panels for the National Autism Project. Her academic background is in social policy analysis and she has a thorough working knowledge of professional practice issues in both adult and children's services. She is autistic, a parent of autistic children and is deeply involved in the adult self-advocate community, having recently retired after many years as company secretary of Autscape. Her website is www.consultyo.com

Dr Libby Gaskell

Libby Gaskell is a chartered counselling psychologist, who has experience of supporting children, adults, and families with a variety of mental health issues and difficulties, across a range of settings. In addition, Libby has delivered lectures to both undergraduate and postgraduate students of psychology and counselling psychology. Libby is an honorary member of Glyndwr University, having a keen interest to pursue research into the areas of therapeutic rehabilitation for those who have offended, and particularly those with a learning disability. Libby currently works in a specialist residential setting for adolescents with sexually harmful or inappropriate behaviours, and alongside which holds a small caseload of clients at a private clinic.

Dr Katie Gaudion

Katie Gaudion is a freelance design consultant and senior research associate at The Helen Hamlyn Centre for Design. Katie's design work celebrates neurodiversity and in a long-term partnership with the autism charity The Kingwood Trust, her research explores how design can improve living environments for autistic adults across the spectrum. Katie has worked within a range of contexts, for example supported living, workplace, gardens, built environment, sensory environments and medium secure hospital ward environments.

An important aspect of Katie's work is to explore new and creative ways to collaborate with autistic people to ensure they are at the centre of the design process. During her PhD Katie created a framework that supports a more positive and personalised design approach, termed 'the triad of strengths'. The framework supports the idea that by understanding a person's sensory preferences, interests and action capabilities, an important palette of ingredients is created that can inform the design of environments, products and services that enhance positive experiences for that person.

Katie's research hopes to expand the field of inclusive design to consider neurodiversity and encourage more designers to collaborate with people who are neurodivergent, who can offer unique perspectives and ideas for innovation that are excluded from mainstream ways of thinking.

Professor Chris Hatton

Chris Hatton is an academic at the Centre for Disability Research, Lancaster University. He has been involved in research, mainly concerning people with learning disabilities and mainly concerned with the inequalities people experience, for over 25 years. He is also currently co-director of the Public Health England Learning Disabilities Observatory.

Joanna Krupa

Joanna Krupa was a social worker for 14 years, working in a team for adults with learning disabilities, having trained following a brief period working in publishing. She then returned to studying and gained a Masters in Social Research in 2015. She is currently a part-time research assistant at London South Bank University.

Dr Joseph Long

Joseph Long is research manager at Scottish Autism where he leads a programme of practice-focused research in social care and education services. The role draws on extensive experience working in autism and learning disability services across the UK. A social anthropologist by training, Joseph is honorary research fellow at the University of Aberdeen and an associate of the Edinburgh Centre for Medical Anthropology. He is also a trustee of HealthProm, an organization dedicated to supporting vulnerable children and families in Russia, Eastern Europe and Central Asia.

Gillian Loomes

Gillian Loomes is currently completing her PhD (a socio-legal study of the Mental Capacity Act 2005) in the Department of Sociology, University of York.

She has a degree in English law and European Law, a PG Cert in special education (autism), a PGDipEd (Advanced PGCE) in lifelong learning, and an MA in social research. She also has a professional background as a specialist autism advocate.

Gillian's research experience includes working with the International Disability Rights Monitor, where she acted as UK researcher on the Regional Report on Europe (published in 2007), and as consultant for the Autism Education Trust. She currently holds a teaching fellowship with the Autism Centre for Education and Research (ACER) at the University of Birmingham.

Gillian is a convener of the Participatory Autism Research Collective (PARC). You can follow her on Twitter - @gillloomes.

Professor Nicola Martin

Nicola Martin joined London South Bank University (LSBU) in 2013 from the London School of Economics and Political Science (LSE), where she took a lead on disability equality. Nicola is professor of education at LSBU and has lead responsibility for the Education Research Centre, with its focus on equality, diversity and social justice. She is a national teaching fellow and has expertise in inclusive practice in education across the age range, critical disability studies and critical autism studies.

Nicola is editor of *The Journal of Inclusive Practice in Further and Higher Education* and former chair of The National Association of Disability Practitioners. She is an honorary visiting fellow at The University of Cambridge and Sheffield Hallam University, a former visiting professor at Hong Kong Institute of Education and a fellow of the RSA. Nicola is principal investigator in a collaborative project with Cambridge University and Research Autism, which explores good practice in mentoring autistic adults.

Prior to LSE Nicola was principal lecturer for inclusive practice and director of the Autism Centre at Sheffield Hallam University. She had a long career at Derby fulfilling various roles, including university principal tutor, head of school and head of division in the Centre for Access and Lifelong Learning. Prior to working in HE Nicola taught disabled learners in schools, clinical settings and FE.

Dr Michael McCreadie

Michael McCreadie is a HCPC registered practitioner psychologist. Michael's clinical practice is primarily in Scotland where he consults in neuro-developmental conditions and he is also a clinician for Studio III clinical services. Michael is a specialist trainer in mindfulness, stress reduction techniques and challenging behaviour. Other appointments include: advisor to Young Scotland in Mind; teaching associate at the National Centre of Autism Studies, University of Strathclyde; research associate, Centre for Practice Innovation, Scottish Autism.

Professor Richard Mills

Richard Mills is the research director for Research Autism and honorary research fellow at the Centre for Applied Autism Research, Department of Psychology, University of Bath. He is also senior research fellow at CASD, Bond University, Australia, editor of *Autism, The International Journal of Research and Practice* and editorial board member of *Advances in Autism*. He was previously with the National Autistic Society as director of research and director of services.

Dr Damian Milton

Damian works part time for the National Autistic Society (NAS) as head of autism knowledge and expertise (adults and community) and sits on the scientific and advisory committee for Research Autism. Damian also teaches on the MA Education (Autism) programme at London South Bank University and has been a consultant for the Transform Autism Education (TAE) project and a number of projects for the Autism Education Trust (AET). In the summer of 2017 Damian joined the Tizard Centre, University of Kent as a part-time lecturer to coincide with his work for the NAS. Damian's interest in autism began when his son was diagnosed in 2005 as autistic at the age of two. Damian was also diagnosed with Asperger's in 2009 at the age of thirty-six.

Dr Dinah Murray

Dinah Murray is an independent researcher and campaigner, former tutor for Birmingham University's distance learning courses on autism (adults) and former support worker for people with varied learning disabilities, including autism. Tutoring involved reading and critiquing hundreds of practitioner research projects. Her work has been published in *Autism*, in *Good Autism Practice* and in a number of books and online. She has presented at numerous conferences (worldwide) on varied themes related to autism, including several years of Autscape, an annual conference-cum-retreat run by and for autistic people. Her autism-related research interests have included: medication and its impact on quality of life, information technology for people who don't use speech, the ethics of autism research and the nature of the human being, with a particular focus on interests. She has been assessed as on the autism spectrum, and if growing up today would certainly have attracted an autism diagnosis.

Professor Sarah Parsons

Sarah Parsons is professor of autism and inclusion, and director of research for Southampton Education School, at the University of Southampton. She has significant research experience in disability related projects and particular interests in the use of innovative technologies for children with autism, evidence-based practices in autism, and research ethics. Sarah has recently established the Autism Community Research Network at Southampton (ACoRNS): http://acornsnetwork.org.uk/).

Professor Elizabeth Pellicano

Elizabeth Pellicano trained as an educational psychologist in Perth, Australia, where she also completed her PhD on the cognitive profile of autistic children, before becoming a junior research fellow in psychiatry at the University of Oxford, UK, and lecturer in experimental psychology at the University of Bristol, UK. In 2009, Liz was appointed senior lecturer at the Centre for Research in Autism and Education (CRAE) at UCL Institute of Education, University College London, UK. She became director of CRAE in 2013 and professor of autism education in 2015. In 2017, Liz returned to Australia to take up the appointment of professor in the Department of Educational Studies at Macquarie University.

An internationally-regarded experimental psychologist, she is also committed to understanding the distinctive opportunities and challenges faced by autistic children, young people and adults, and tracing their impact on everyday life – at home, at school and out-and-about in the community. She has been consistently dedicated both to enhancing public understanding of autism, its challenges and opportunities, and to ensuring that autistic people and their allies have greater involvement in the decisions that ultimately affect them, including in the research process.

Dr Susy Ridout

Susy Ridout comes from a background encompassing arts, health and education working in the UK, Cuba and Spain. Here she has initiated and run a number of disability dance and art-based projects, which led her to further pursue her concern about the exclusion of autistic people from decision making about key aspects of their lives. As such, she has recently completed her doctorate at the University of Birmingham exploring methods to bring autistic voices to the fore in research and service provision. She has been active as a mentor and academic skills support worker with autistic and disabled people both within and outside higher education establishments for the last seven years. In addition, she contributes to HE courses relating to autism and has presented on issues around autism, epilepsy and well-being at conferences including Autscape and more recently the ESRC research seminar series: *Shaping Autism Research in the UK*. Susy is neurodivergent.

Dr Peter Vermeulen

Peter Vermeulen has an MSc and PhD in psychology and educational sciences and has worked with people with ASD and their families for more than 25 years. He previously worked for the Flemish Autism Association, first as home trainer for families with a child with autism, later as director of the home training centre and finally as trainer/lecturer. He is now co-director of Autisme Centraal, a training and education centre for autism spectrum disorders in Belgium. Peter is an internationally respected lecturer/trainer presenting all over Europe and beyond and has written more than 15 books and several articles on autism.

Dr Mitzi Waltz

Mitzi Waltz is docent in public health at Vrije Universiteit Amsterdam and a senior researcher in disability studies in The Netherlands. She has researched and written extensively about supporting and educating people with autism, and has a particular interest in policies and practices that facilitate independent living. She studied architecture and planning at the University of New Mexico from 1980-1984.

Editorial

Dr Damian Milton and Professor Nicola Martin

This collection has been brought to you by a highly creative group of people, many of whom are either on the autism spectrum or have close family ties to autistic people. The focus of this annual is not on the causes of autism, and the editors and authors herein certainly do not subscribe to the 'cure autism now' school of thought. Our interest lies in considering ways in which autistic people (focusing here on those with additional intellectual impairments) can have the best possible quality of life, on their own terms.

While this publication is aimed at health and social care professionals we do not subscribe to the view that autistic people just need to be 'looked after'. We are interested in lifelong education, employment, relationships, independent living, creative expression, leisure and everything else that makes life rich. This volume scratches the surface and traces some key concerns across the adult life course from school leaving to old age. Common themes emerge between authors, including the fundamental requirement to acknowledge and respect and facilitate autistic expertise as central to the production of research, policy and practice. We are grateful to The Participatory Autism Research Collective (PARC) for their role as autistic experts in contributing to the production and review of this volume.

Our focus on respect for and well-being of autistic people is demonstrated by the underpinning assumption, which runs as a thread through this work, that it is necessary to understand the world view of an individual in order to assist them effectively. For people who do not communicate in conventional ways, practitioners, policy makers and researchers need to step up to the challenge of ensuring that these views are heard and respected.

This annual collection rejects terminology such as 'challenging behaviour' and 'obsessive interests' in favour of the ethos of empathically understanding the autistic person and what it is that an individual feels troubled or passionate about. These understandings are vital in order to develop inclusive environments in which people can articulate their preferences and aspirations and realise their potential.

In this second volume, there is a substantial focus on autistic people with intellectual impairments who come into contact with the criminal justice system, with three chapters on this topic. Other topics include employment, autism and intellectual impairment in old age, mental health, housing, and the transforming care agenda. We have also included a number of chapters on our continuing theme of participatory research and practice.

Editorial

The whole area of social interaction and 'empathy', in all its variety, merits deeper consideration and this is something which could be the focus of a future volume. We hope you find our approach useful and interesting and that what you read here will impact on your practice in ways which directly benefit autistic people.

If you are interested in submitting to future volumes of the annual, please email Damian Milton at d.e.m.milton-2@kent.ac.uk for more information.

Section I:
Policy and campaigns

Autistic people and Transforming Care: what do we know?

Professor Chris Hatton

Abstract

After the exposure of abusive practices in a 'specialist' inpatient unit for people with learning disabilities or autistic people, one of the aims of the Transforming Care programme in England has been to reduce the number of these units and the number of people contained within them.

Although statistics suggest the total number of people in these units is very slowly reducing over time, the number of people labelled as autistic in these statistics is increasing. Statistics also suggest that autistic people are more likely to be in general mental health inpatient units compared to people with learning disabilities.

Beyond this, there is very little statistical information about autistic people in these inpatient units, although one study reported that autistic people were more likely to be subject to physical restraint than people with learning disabilities. As a result, the Transforming Care programme is somewhat misdirected when it comes to understanding and supporting the diverse community of autistic people in England, and does not address the obstacles to accessing decent healthcare experienced by autistic people.

Introduction

In May 2011, the BBC documentary programme Panorama broadcast an undercover expose of shocking abusive practices at Winterbourne View, near Bristol in England, a 'specialist' inpatient unit for autistic people or people with learning disabilities, supposedly designed to assess and support people in distress or crisis. As a result of the public response, the UK government, mainly through NHS England (the agency responsible for directing health services in England), has set a national policy goal of trying to drastically reduce the number of people in these specialist inpatient units (around 2,500 to 3,000 places taken up at the moment). This policy is called Transforming Care (NHS England 2015a, 2015b, 2015c). More recently this policy aim has been accompanied by plans to improve services for people outside of these units, so that people are less likely to reach points of crisis in the first place and are more likely to be supported outside of inpatient units when they do reach crisis point.

Since the Panorama programme, there have been more shocking examples of poor practice in these units, including the preventable death of Connor Sparrowhawk (see the #JusticeforLB campaign: http://justiceforlb.org/), and it is unclear what impact national policy is having.

National policy consistently talks about 'people with learning disabilities and/or autism' as the focus of Transforming Care, although this phrase encompasses an incredibly diverse group of people. This chapter looks at what we know specifically about autistic people within inpatient services and the Transforming Care programme more generally.

How many autistic people are in 'specialist' inpatient services?

The first, most basic question to ask is how many autistic people are in the 'specialist' inpatient services covered by Transforming Care? These inpatient services include Assessment and Treatment Units (ATUs), other 'specialist' higher security inpatient units for people with learning disabilities or autistic people, and inpatient services for anyone with a mental health problem.

Figure 1 shows numbers from the Learning Disability Census for 2013, 2014 and 2015 (NHS Digital, 2015; 2016). In these years, the census asked all services providing these kinds of inpatient care for information on who was in their service on 30th September and what was happening to them. As part of the information requested, service providers were asked to categorise everyone in their inpatient services into one of four categories: learning disabilities only, autism only, learning disabilities and autism, neither autism nor learning disabilities. **Figure 1** shows the number of people in inpatient services in these four categories for 2013, 2014 and 2015.

→ **Figure 1** shows that according to the Learning Disability Census the total number of people in these inpatient services dropped slightly, from 3,250 people in 2013 to 3,000 people in 2015, a drop of 8%.

→ The number of people categorised as learning disabilities also decreased over this time period, from 1,919 people in 2013 to 1,660 people in 2015 (a drop of 13%).

→ The number of people categorised as learning disabilities and autism also fell, from 908 people in 2013 to 710 people in 2015 (a drop of 22%).

→ However, the number of people categorised as having only autism increased by almost half, from 308 people in 2013 to 455 people in 2015 (a rise of 48%).

Figure 1: Number of people (categorised as learning disabilities only, autism only, learning disabilities and autism, neither) in 'specialist' inpatient services in 2013, 2014 and 2015 (source: Learning Disability Census (NHS Digital, 2015; 2016))

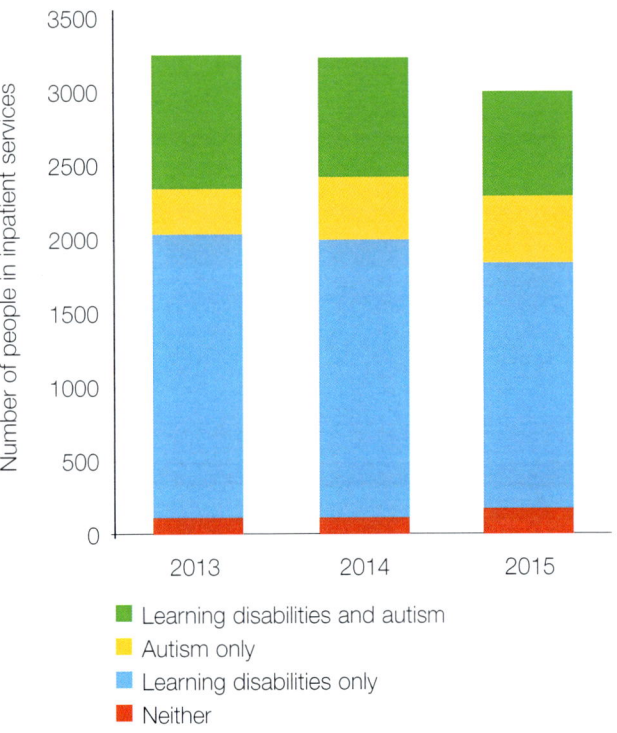

→ According to health service commissioners, the total number of people in these inpatient services dropped from 2,615 people in March 2016 to 2,590 people in March 2017, a drop of 5%.

→ The number of people categorised as learning disabilities only in inpatient services dropped from 1,520 people in March 2016 to 1,395 people in March 2017, a drop of 8% that continues the earlier trend reported from 2013 to 2015.

→ The number of people categorised as learning disabilities and autism increased slightly, from 560 people in March 2016 to 570 people in March 2017, an increase of 2%, reversing the earlier trend from 2013 to 2015.

→ The number of people categorised as autism only continued to increase, from 435 people in March 2016 to 455 people in March 2017, an increase of 5%.

Figure 2: Number of people (categorised as learning disabilities only, autism only, learning disabilities and autism, neither) in 'specialist' inpatient services from March 2016 to March 2017 (source: NHS Digital Assuring Transformation data)

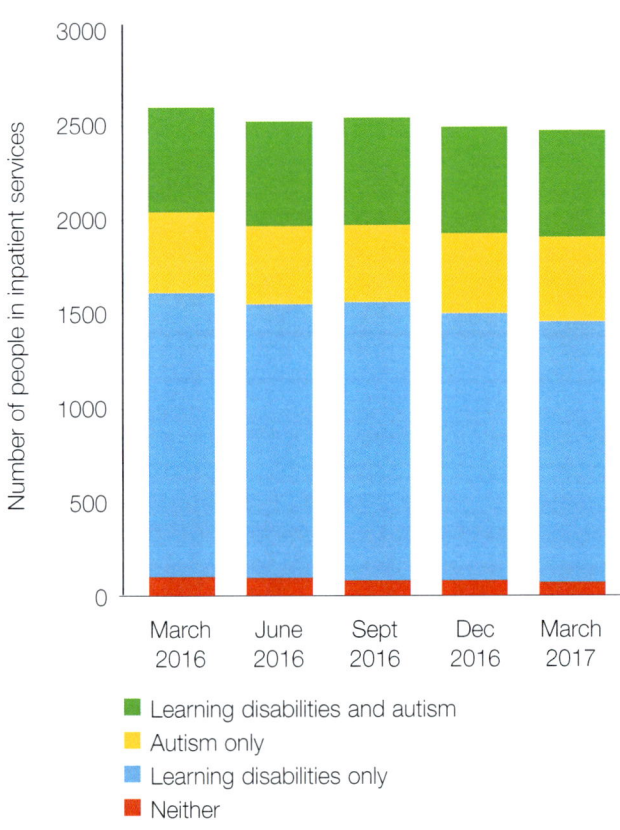

The Learning Disability Census was stopped in 2015 and there are no plans to repeat it. However, the same four categories are used in another more recent source of information published by NHS Digital that tracks monthly the number of people in similar 'specialist' inpatient services (NHS Digital, 2017a). This information comes from the more than 200 organisations in England that use public money to commission (i.e. buy) health services, including inpatient services. Almost all of these are clinical commissioning groups that are supposed to plan and commission services to meet the health needs of everyone in their local area. A small number of these organisations are part of NHS England, and commission 'specialist' mental health and other services on a regional (rather than local) basis. Commissioners consistently report lower numbers of people in these 'specialist' inpatient services compared to the Learning Disability Census, for reasons that aren't completely clear.

Figure 2 shows the number of people in inpatient services at three-monthly intervals from March 2016 to March 2017 according to commissioners, using the same four categories as reported in the census.

Taken together, this information shows that both the number and proportion of autistic people (according to these service categorisations) in these specialist inpatient units is increasing. This is particularly true for people put into the category of autism only (i.e. without a learning disability) – as of March 2017 18% of all people in these inpatient units were in this category. Added to the 23% of people in these inpatient services put into the learning disabilities and autism category, this means that over 40% of people in specialist inpatient services are, according to services, autistic people.

Inpatient services themselves have been classified into a number of types depending on their apparent purpose, the level of security imposed on people within them, and whether they are catering for people who have committed offences. Statistics are reported on how many people are in different types of inpatient service, but they are not generally published according to the learning disability and/or autism categories discussed above. This means we have very little information on where autistic people are. One snippet of information is from the 2015 Learning Disability Census, which reported that:

→ For people in the category of learning disabilities only, the vast majority of people (1,305 people, 79%) were in learning disability wards, with relatively few people in mental health wards (330 people, 20%) and even fewer in 'other' wards (25 people, 1%).

→ Figures were similar for people in the category of learning disabilities and autism, with 85% of people (605 people) in learning disability wards, 12% of people (85 people) in mental health wards and 3% of people (20 people) in 'other' wards.

→ The picture for people in the category of autism only was quite different. Here, less than half of people (170 people, 38%) were in learning disability wards, just over half of people (240 people, 53%) were in mental health wards and 9% of people (40 people) were in 'other' wards.

This information suggests that autistic people without a learning disability are more likely to be in general mental health inpatient wards/units, while autistic people with learning disabilities are overwhelmingly likely to be in learning disability wards/units.

The newest source of statistical information on mental health services for people with learning disabilities and autistic people is the Mental Health Services Monthly Statistics produced by NHS Digital (NHS Digital, 2017b). This produces information on all people identified by services as a person with learning disabilities or an autistic person using any inpatient mental health service, not just 'specialist' inpatient units. Unfortunately this dataset does not differentiate between people with learning disabilities and autistic people in any of its reporting, instead putting everyone into an 'LDA' group. However, it does report a high number of people in the LDA group using adult mental health inpatient services (1,410 people in ward stays at the end of March 2017). How many of these people are autistic? This is particularly worrying as very few local areas say that they offer good crisis support to autistic people without learning disabilities (Mehta et al, 2017).

What happens to autistic people in inpatient services?

So far, the statistics have shown that the number of autistic people in inpatient services is increasing while the overall numbers are static or slightly decreasing, and that autistic people without an additional learning disability label are more likely to be in general adult mental health inpatient wards/units rather than 'specialist' learning disability wards/units.

What do the statistics tell us about why autistic people end up in these inpatient services, how long they are in them, and what happens to them when they are there? The answer is straightforward – in their published form statistics don't tell us anything specific about the circumstances of autistic people compared to people with learning disabilities in inpatient services.

In general, the statistics tell us that specialist inpatient services for people with learning disabilities or autistic people are not good places to be, are not succeeding even on their own terms, and are not reducing in number at the pace set by national Transforming Care policy (NHS England 2015a). We know very little about the experiences of people with learning disabilities or autistic people in general mental health inpatient units.

So, for people with learning disabilities or autistic people in specialist inpatient services at the end of March 2017 we know:

→ 200 young people aged under 18 years old were in inpatient services.

→ Nearly half of people (49%) had been admitted to their current inpatient unit from an acute hospital bed.

→ People had spent on average almost three years (1,027 days) in their current inpatient unit, and over five years (1,958 days) continuously in inpatient units (including transfers directly between units).

→ 30% of people in inpatient services did not need inpatient care according to their care plan.

→ 59% of people in inpatient services had no planned date for transfer from their unit.

(NHS Digital, 2017a)

Based on the most recent information we have, from the 2015 Learning Disability Census:

→ 18% of people in specialist inpatient services (530 people) had experienced an accident in the three months before the census, with 10 people experiencing more than 10 accidents in this period.

→ 23% of people (665 people) had been physically assaulted in the previous three months, with 45 people assaulted more than 20 times in this period.

→ 24% of people (735 people) had experienced self-harm in the previous three months, 45 people experiencing self-harm on more than 20 occasions in this period.

→ Almost half of people in specialist inpatient units (46%) had experienced an accident, a physical assault, and/or self-harm in the three months before the census.

→ 13% of people (380 people) had experienced being put into seclusion at least once in the previous three months, with 15 people being subject to seclusion more than 20 times in this period.

→ 34% of people (1,030 people) had experienced at least one episode of hands-on restraint in the previous three months, with 115 people being subject to physical restraint more than 20 times in this period.

→ Almost three-quarters of people (2,155 people, 72%) in inpatient units had received antipsychotic medication in the 28 days before the census, with almost all of these people (2,025) getting antipsychotics on a regular basis.

→ 11% of people (320 people) had been subject to rapid tranquilisation medication in the last 28 days.

What are the circumstances and experiences of inpatient autistic people with or without learning disabilities specifically?

We know very little, although one analysis of older inpatient census data reported that 'Autism was associated with a 25% increase in use of restraint' (Glover & Olson, 2012, p33).

Campaigning groups of families of people with learning disabilities or autistic people in inpatient units often talk about how bad these inpatient services are, including how services don't understand autistic people (7 Days of Action, 2016; Bringing Us Together 2016a, 2016b) and cause people and families real harm. However, direct accounts of autistic people's experiences of inpatient services seem to be pretty absent (Baines & Hatton 2017; NDTi, 2015).

Conclusion: the invisibility of autistic people in Transforming Care policy

The statistics that have been publicly reported show that large and increasing numbers of autistic people with and without learning disabilities in England are being detained in the types of specialist inpatient services covered by Transforming Care, figures that are supposed to be reducing. There are also some hints that large numbers of autistic people are spending time in generic mental health inpatient services. Beyond that, the publicly available statistics report very little about the specific circumstances and experiences of autistic people in the types of specialist inpatient service covered by Transforming Care, and even less about what's happening to autistic people in generic mental health inpatient services.

Instead, people with learning disabilities and autistic people are treated in the statistics as one homogeneous group. This is also consistently the case in Transforming Care policy, where the foundational documents (NHS England 2015a; 2015b; 2015c) very rarely specifically mention autism, almost exclusively referring to people with a learning disability and/ or autism. In practice, this has resulted in the Transforming Care programme being somewhat misdirected when it comes to understanding and supporting the diverse community of autistic people in England, and does not address the obstacles to accessing decent healthcare experienced by autistic people (Westminster Commission on Autism, 2016).

References

7 Days of Action (2016) *Autumn 2016: Human* [online]. Available at: https://www.sevendaysofaction.net/our-campaigns/autumn-2016-human/ (accessed September 2017).

Baines S & Hatton C (eds) (2017) *Autism Self-Assessment Exercise 2016: Personal stories*. London: Public Health England. Available at: https://www.gov.uk/government/publications/autism-self-assessment-framework-exercise (accessed September 2017).

Bringing Us Together (2016a) *Stronger Together – Family event*. Bringing Us Together website.

Bringing Us Together (2016b) *Stronger Together – Families talk about their experience of independent hospitals*. Bringing Us Together website.

Glover G & Olsen F (2012) *Assessment and Treatment Units and Other Specialist Inpatient Care for People with Learning Disabilities in the Count-Me-In surveys, 2006-2010* [online]. Durham: Improving Health and Lives Learning Disabilities Observatory. Available at: http://webarchive.nationalarchives.gov.uk/20160704150527/http://improvinghealthandlives.org.uk/uploads/doc/vid_17542_IHAL%202012-09%20A%26T%20and%20other%20specialist%20inpatient%20care%20for%20people%20with%20LD%20in%20the%20Count-Me-In%20Census.pdf (accessed September 2017).

Mehta H, Thackeray A, Khundakar K, Baines S, Glover G & Hatton C (2017) *Autism Self-Assessment Exercise 2016: Detailed report and thematic analysis* [online]. London: Public Health England. Available at: https://www.gov.uk/government/publications/autism-self-assessment-framework-exercise (accessed September 2017).

National Development Team for Inclusion (NDTi) (2015) *Informing the Service Model: A report about the experiences of people with learning disabilities and families.* Bath: NDTi.

NHS Digital (2015) *Learning Disability Census Report – England, 30th of September 2015* [online]. Leeds: NHS Digital. Available at: http://content.digital.nhs.uk/catalogue/PUB19428 (accessed September 2017).

NHS Digital (2016) Learning Disability Census Report. Learning Disabilities Census Report – Further Analysis: England, 30 September 2015. Leeds: NHS Digital. Available at: https://www.gov.uk/government/statistics/learning-disabilities-census-report-further-analysis-england-30-sep-2015 (accessed September 2017).

NHS Digital (2017a) Learning Disability Services Monthly Statistics – England Commissioner Census (Assuring Transformation) – April 2017, Provisional Statistics. Leeds: NHS Digital. http://www.content.digital.nhs.uk/catalogue/PUB24101 (accessed September 2017).

NHS Digital (2017b) *Mental Health Services Monthly Statistics: Final, March 2017* [online]. Learning disabilities and autism reference tables. Leeds: NHS Digital. Available at: http://www.digital.nhs.uk/catalogue/PUB30000 (accessed September 2017).

NHS England (2015a) *Transforming Care for People with Learning Disabilities: The next steps*. London: NHS England. Available at: https://www.england.nhs.uk/wp-content/uploads/2015/01/transform-care-nxt-stps.pdf (accessed September 2017).

NHS England (2015b) *Building the Right Support: A national plan to develop community services and close inpatient facilities for people with a learning disability and/or autism who display behaviour that challenges, including those with a mental health condition* [online]. London: NHS England. Available at: https://www.england.nhs.uk/wp-content/uploads/2015/10/ld-nat-imp-plan-oct15.pdf (accessed September 2017).

NHS England (2015c) *Supporting People with a Learning Disability and/ or Autism who Display Behaviour that Challenges, including those with a Mental Health Condition: Service model for commissioners of health and social care services* [online]. London: NHS England. Available at: https://www.england.nhs.uk/wp-content/uploads/2015/10/service-model-291015.pdf (accessed September 2017).

Westminster Commission on Autism (2016) *A Spectrum of Obstacles: An inquiry into access to healthcare for autistic people.* London: Westminster Commission on Autism. Available at: https://westminsterautismcommission.files.wordpress.com/2016/03/ar1011_ncg-autism-report-july-2016.pdf (accessed September 2017).

Challenging the ideology of idealised normalcy

Dr Damian EM Milton

Abstract

The history of autism has been beset by controversies over what exactly autism is, and how best to support autistic people in society. In this chapter, notions of normalcy are critically reflected upon in relation to current models of practice for autistic adults with additional learning disabilities in support services. This includes a critique of the dominant model-informing practice in this area currently; that of positive behaviour support (PBS), and the common theoretical assumptions underpinning the notion of 'challenging behaviour' and how to best 'manage' it. This chapter argues for a more eclectic approach to support that encompasses theories of cognition, subjectivity, action, and social life, which are often left unaccounted for in a simplistic implementation of a PBS model based within a framework of idealising 'normalcy'.

Introduction

If one looks at how autism is diagnosed and subsequently 'treated', one can see that autism is defined as a developmental 'disorder', a deviation away from the 'typical' development that one might expect, deemed to be in need of remedial intervention to acquire as much 'normality' as possible. Such a focus compares autistic development against the statistical ideal of the norm, with abnormal ways of being observed and classified as 'maladaptive behaviours'. 'Adaptive behaviour' or 'functioning' relates to:

> '...the relative ability of a person to effectively interact with society on all levels and care for one's self; affected by one's willingness to practice skills and pursue opportunities for improvement on all levels. Often used to describe levels of mental retardation.'

(Online Medical Dictionary, 2017).

Therefore, from the outset, autism is viewed as primarily a childhood (developmental) disorder or deviancy from expected 'typical' development, which adversely affects a person's ability to effectively interact with society 'independently'. Improvement is framed as individual responsibility to strive toward normalcy. When autism itself is defined in terms of behavioural dysfunction from the norm, perhaps it is little wonder that much research and practice is based on medicalised remedial models of what it means to support an autistic person and improve their quality of life.

For the purposes of this chapter, I have chosen to reference the PBS competency framework (Positive Behaviour Academy, 2017) as a way of highlighting the ethos behind the implementation of this model and some of the issues that ensue from doing so.

Positive behaviour support (PBS)

> 'It is based on the assessment of the broad social and physical context in which the behaviour occurs, and used to construct socially valid interventions which enhance quality of life outcomes for both the person themselves and their carers.'

(Positive Behaviour Academy, 2017, p6).

This quote indicates the philosophy behind the functional assessment of behaviour, looking at the antecedents (broad social and physical context) and consequences (social valid interventions). Yet one can see that quality of life is being framed in terms of being 'socially valid'. One could perhaps trace a connection with the work of Wolf Wolfensburger (1972) on 'normalisation', where it was suggested that people with intellectual impairments needed to be moved out of institutional care. A laudable aim, and yet he suggested that stigmatising attitudes towards those with intellectual impairments could be reduced by creating opportunities to take on social roles, in what was called 'social role valorisation'. This was envisaged to help increase the social value of people with intellectual impairments, and challenge the perception that such people were completely 'other'. Aspects of this approach have been widely criticised by scholars of critical disability studies, as it could be said they rely too heavily on societal norms that are already disabling.

> 'PBS combines the technology of behavioural intervention with the values of normalisation, human rights, and self-determination to deliver effective person-centred support for people whose behaviour challenges. Crucially, these values inform both the way in which this technology is used and the outcomes that it is designed to achieve.'

(Positive Behaviour Academy, 2017, p6).

The key components of a PBS approach and values are shown in the following list (Gore et al, 2013, cited in Positive Behaviour Academy, 2017, p7):

'*Values*:

1. *Prevention and reduction of challenging behaviour occurs within the context of increased quality of life, inclusion, participation, and the defence and support of valued social roles.*
2. *Constructional approaches to intervention design build stakeholder skills and opportunities, and reject aversive and restrictive practices.*
3. *Stakeholder participation informs, implements, and validates assessment and intervention practices.*

Theory and evidence base:

4. *An understanding that challenging behaviour develops to serve important functions for people.*
5. *The primary use of constructional principles and procedures from behaviour analysis to assess and support behaviour change.*
6. *The secondary use of other complementary, evidence-based approaches to support behaviour change at multiple levels of a system.*

Processes:

7. *A data-driven approach to decision making at every stage.*
8. *Functional assessment to inform function-based intervention.*
9. *Multi-component interventions to change behaviour (proactively) and manage behaviour (reactively).*
10. *Implementation support, monitoring and evaluation of interventions over the long term.*'

From the values described in the PBS competency framework, one can see that quality of life is associated with the prevention and reduction of 'challenging behaviour' and an increase in community participation, yet is framed normatively. Aversive and restrictive practices are rejected (although often perhaps utilised in practice), yet the approach is said to be 'constructional' and designed to build 'skills':

> '*PBS interventions are also constructional in that increasing the person's repertoire of adaptive behaviours and their range of positive life opportunities is a central objective. In contrast, the use of aversive or punitive interventions is rejected on the basis of their incompatibility with a values-led approach.*'

(Positive Behaviour Academy, 2017, p6).

Within such an ideological framing, one's opportunities for positive social experiences are seen as dependent on one's repertoire of 'adaptive' (normative) behaviours. Such a values base is one entrenched within neo-liberal ideals of individual responsibility and highly dubious when looked at from the standpoint of the social model of disability (Milton, 2012a) which locates disablement within social structures and cultures. It is also doubtful that all learning can be framed as a set of explicit skills, but requires ongoing tacit engagement (Milton, 2014a; Milton, 2014b).

In terms of 'theory and evidence-base' and 'process', the framework talks about 'behaviour change' and also the importance of understanding the 'function' of behaviour. Within this model, the writing of a behaviour support plan requires the 'sound knowledge' of behavioural techniques and functional assessments. In this ideology, behaviours serve 'functions' (or purposes) for an individual, but as they are deemed to be challenging to either themselves and/or other people, there may be ways of teaching new skills or behaviours which serve the same function, yet are deemed less 'challenging'. Yet it is this contrived and reductionist account of the purposes of behaviour which is one of the models biggest flaws.

The following list shows guidance advice from the PBS Competency Framework (Positive Behaviour Academy, 2017, p43):

- '*That behaviour happens for a reason and that our collective role is to understand what that purpose is.*
- *That all behaviour (apart from reflexes) is learned and that an understanding of how behaviour is learned can be used to teach new skills.*
- *The 4-term contingency: motivation, antecedents, behaviour, and consequences (definitions, dimensions, relationships between).*
- *The 4 common functions of challenging behaviour: social attention, avoidance/escape, access to tangibles, sensory stimulation.*
- *The difference between the form (what a behaviour looks like) and its function.*
- *Identify and clearly describe behaviour and environmental antecedents in observable and measurable terms (distinguishes between judgements and descriptions).*
- *Identify and report other variables that might affect the person (e.g. illness, relocation, medication).*
- *Recognise the effect of own behaviour on the person and adapt accordingly.*'

Do all actions have discernible reasons? Or are these post-event rationalisations? If 'function' is not 'intent', then what is it really referring to? Surely some actions are unintentional and not just in regards to the consequences of action. Is all action 'learnt', or are all actions occurring in a present, perhaps attempting to simulate past actions, but performed idiosyncratically anew? It is good to see the model move beyond the 'ABC' of functional assessment to include 'motivation', but why is the focus often on the 'behaviour' and the 'consequence' (e.g. reinforcement), rather than averting the causes of distress, the 'motivations' and 'antecedents'? Maybe, 'Positive support focused on motivation and antecedent analysis within social contexts' doesn't have the same ring to it?

When one looks at the four 'functions' of 'challenging behaviour', one can see a distinct lack of depth as to why people may be acting in a certain way. When someone has a bout of 'road rage', is this to gain social attention, avoidance, to access tangibles, or for sensory stimulation? The answer would be none of the above. If this is true of the 'challenging behaviour' of non-autistic people, it can be equally true of autistic people.

In analysing the antecedents of an action, the variables are so numerous one could say a scientific analysis of them is constrained to say the least. This means that interpretations of observed antecedents and behaviours may be simply incorrect. Given the breakdown in mutual reciprocity often found in interactions between autistic and non-autistic people (Milton, 2012b), one could say this is indeed more than likely to occur in practice. It would then follow that practitioners should be extremely humble and reflective in their interpretations and consequential actions. Yet, to what extent is such space available to staff working with autistic adults with additional learning disabilities?

Whilst it is true that PBS is not the only approach infused with the idealisation of normalcy that is used with autistic adults, it is a clear and often used example. Interestingly, in research I carried out to look into educational ideology and autistic children (Milton, 2016), although non-autistic parents of autistic children were largely in favour of an educational approach approximating PBS, the motivation for this was not normalisation. Instead, parents often wanted to build resilience in their children in the face of a discriminatory society. The autistic adults surveyed were generally against the approach, and instead prioritised celebrating diversity. This calls into question autism research that uses normative outcomes as measures of success or quality of life. Also, perhaps it is not autistic people, but those that target autistic people for abuse who are more in need of such interventions?

Challenging behaviour

One of the most problematic areas in regard to practice models and an example of the damaging narrative of the idealisation of normalcy is in the application of the notion of 'challenging behaviour', traditionally defined as:

> 'Culturally abnormal behaviour(s) of such an intensity, frequency or duration that the physical safety of the person or others is likely to be placed in serious jeopardy, or behaviour which is likely to seriously limit use of, or result in the person being denied access to, ordinary community facilities.'

(Emerson, 1995, cited by the Challenging Behaviour Foundation, 2017).

When a person's actions put themselves or others in jeopardy, I would not wish to argue with those wanting to find a way to intervene (if safely, ethically, and in an informed way). Yet, the beginning and end of this well worn quote are far more problematic. Why should it matter is someone's actions are culturally abnormal or not? Is not the denial of community access more to do with society than how someone acts? Or is the social model disregarded when it comes to people deemed to be displaying 'challenging behaviour'? At least, one is left with the question: 'challenging for whom?'

Normalcy and ableism

Since the days of Francis Galton, there have been attempts to categorise people on the basis of intelligence or something equating to 'adaptive functioning', leading to a burgeoning industry around the surveillance of normality and deviance, particularly in regard to childhood development. When looking at the quality of life of autistic adults with additional learning disabilities, one needs to move beyond normative ideology, the application of which leads to ableism (the presumption of non-disabled normality and discrimination against those who do not meet up to such expectations). The critical disability studies scholar Lennard Davis (2010) suggests that through our experiences of non-normativity and marginality, we are given the chance to 'imagine otherwise'. To begin with this process, let me suggest the Pavilion Publishing publication: *Ten Rules for Ensuring People with Learning Disabilities and Those Who are on the Autism Spectrum Develop 'Challenging Behaviour': …and maybe what to do about it* (Milton *et al*, 2016).

References

Challenging Behaviour Foundation (CBF) (2017) *What is Challenging Behaviour?* [online]. Available at: http://www.challengingbehaviour.org.uk/about-us/about-challenging-behaviour/what-is-challenging-behaviour.html (accessed September 2017).

Davis L (Ed) (2010) *The Disability Studies Reader* (third edition). London: Routledge.

Milton D (2012a) *So What Exactly Is Autism?* London: Autism Education Trust.

Milton D (2012b) On the ontological status of autism: the 'double empathy problem'. *Disability and Society* **27** (6) 883–887.

Milton D (2014a) Autistic expertise: a critical reflection on the production of knowledge in autism studies. *Autism: The International Journal of Research and Practice (special issue: Autism and Society)* **18** (7) 794–802.

Milton D (2014b) So what exactly are autism interventions intervening with? *Good Autism Practice* **15** (2) 6–14.

Milton D (2016) *Educational Discourse and the Autistic Student: A study using Q-sort methodology* [doctoral thesis]. Birmingham: University of Birmingham.

Milton D, Mills R & Jones S (2016) *Ten Rules for Ensuring People with Learning Disabilities and Those Who are on the Autism Spectrum Develop 'Challenging Behaviour': …and maybe what to do about it.* Brighton: Pavilion Publishing and Media Ltd.

Online Medical Dictionary (2017). Available at: http://medical-dictionary.thefreedictionary.com/adaptive+functioning (accessed September 2017).

Positive Behaviour Academy (2017) *PBS Competency Framework* [online]. Available at: http://pbsacademy.org.uk/wp-content/uploads/2016/11/Positive-Behavioural-Support-Competence-Framework-May-2015.pdf (accessed September 2017).

Wolfensberger W (1972) *The Principle of Normalization in Human Services*. Toronto: NIMR.

Rethinking housing for people with autism and intellectual disability

Dr Mitzi Waltz

Abstract

People with autism and intellectual disability will typically live in the same community settings as non-disabled people. The right kind of housing can only be determined through individual assessment of needs and preferences. Many people will need a housing package that includes some form of support. Safe, appropriate housing is crucial for successful independent or supported living, however adults with autism face many barriers to obtaining it. These include funding cuts and pressure for (re)institutionalisation. Guidance is easily available for new-build projects, but creative renovation and customisation are easier and less expensive.

Introduction

Since the 1970s, the discussion around housing policy and practice for autistic people and intellectual disability has centred on moving disabled adults from large institutions to community-based housing. While most large institutions in the UK have now closed, the effect has often been to push responsibility for housing onto aging parents, or to replace large institutions with smaller facilities that often replicate similar levels of neglect, abuse, reduction in personal autonomy and choice, and isolation. At the same time, greater understanding about the broader autism spectrum makes it clear that the majority of autistic people do not live in specialist facilities, but in the community. That is as it should be for all, but many autistic individuals need support and assistance with finding, keeping and adapting housing. When support is unavailable, autistic adults can find independence unattainable (Begeer *et al*, 2013), or endure ongoing problems related to housing (Harker & King, 2004; PAS, 2014).

In the UK, fewer than ten percent of autistic adults live independently without formal support. A further eight percent live independently with some formal support, while 33 percent live in specialist housing. Just under half live with parents or another family member (Harker & King, 2004). Few autistic adults are in full-time work, housing benefit levels are low compared to market rents, and social housing is hard to come by (Johns & Cooper *et al*, 2007). More able autistic adults are usually not eligible at all for supported housing schemes, but there is also a severe shortage of safe, supported housing for people with autism and intellectual disabilities (ibid.). These factors, not cultural preferences, account for the low number of British adults with autism in independent living.

For those who live in specialist housing, such as group homes, many are in facilities for people with intellectual disabilities rather than autism-specialist facilities.

The 'Housing First' approach

For autistic people, home represents a potential refuge from sensory overload and interpersonal difficulties. Unfortunately, for many the reality is that an inadequate, inappropriate or insecure housing situation instead creates greater sensory and/or social stress.

Unaffordable housing, unsafe or unhealthy housing, and homelessness are destabilising factors that have far-reaching impacts. These impacts have been recognised and addressed by the 'Housing First' approach pioneered in the US with regards to its large population of homeless people with serious mental illnesses (a group that includes many people with autism, often un- or mis-diagnosed). Housing First-based projects have found that a safe, affordable place to live creates stability that can radiate out into other aspects of life, including managing diet and personal hygiene, mood self-regulation, diminishing problematic use of drugs and alcohol, better overall health, and enhanced ability to form and maintain relationships (Pearson *et al*, 2007). Housing insecurity also contributes to lack of access to work, as disabled tenants feel they cannot risk moving to take a job.

Current challenges

In the current age of austerity, there are pressures to return to institutional placements, and to change institutional conditions in ways that are particularly unfavourable for autistic people. Recent research has found that housing issues frequently top the list of direct impacts from austerity measures, which have been implemented without regard to the rising cost of housing and lack of housing choice. For example, a joint survey by the British Academy of Childhood Disability and the British Association for Community Child Health found that 34 percent of families with disabled children in the UK reported housing issues, including evictions, forced moves, housing that is inadequate for the needs of disabled family members, or becoming homeless (BACCH & BACD, 2015). Paediatricians further reported that most had been approached for help with housing issues, such as support to obtain suitable housing for a family with a disabled child or to be exempted from the 'bedroom tax' (ibid).

Pressure for re-institutionalisation was reported in Romania, Hungary and Ireland in 2012 (Hauben *et al*, 2012); these pressures were also described by United Nations investigators in the United Kingdom (Committee on the Rights of Persons with Disabilities, 2016). In the Netherlands, funding models favour institutional care over independent living, and can have particularly negative consequences for autistic adults (Reindl *et al*, 2016). In Portugal residential care conditions have changed in ways that are likely to negatively impact people with autism in particular—long waiting lists and uncertainty about placement; retention of large institutions because group homes and independent living supports have not been adequately funded; shared bedrooms, and smaller bedrooms (Hauben *et al*, 2012).

Further, several EU states have slashed budgets for independent living support or eliminated existing programmes, including Spain, Ireland and the UK (Hauben *et al*, 2012). Without this support, autistic adults are typically forced to live with aging parents on a long-term basis. This often results in unsuitable emergency placements when family arrangements break down or parents die. Continuing to live with parents beyond the culturally appropriate age for independence limits self-determination and participation in further education, work and adult relationships. It can also have negative impact on the well-being and health of parents (Dykens *et al*, 2014; Piazza *et al*, 2014). When family housing is not suitable for an autistic child or adult, the whole family is faced with serious stresses and extra costs as they try to 'make do.'

Both large and small-scale residential care facilities limit self-determination and community participation (Stancliffe, 2001; Robertson *et al*, 2001). These facilities are almost never designed specifically for autistic people, and rarely provide for customisation to meet individual needs or preferences. Design choices, such as surveillance and security features or durable, easy-to-clean materials, are typically made to suit staff priorities.

Key principles for effective alternatives

Housing is enshrined as an essential human right (United Nations High Commissioner for Human Rights, 2014), and housing that is suitable for people with disabilities should be advocated for in that context. In addition, housing that presents barriers for autistic people (for example, high levels of noise or lack of control over social contact) is disabling. These issues should be seen as disability access factors, just as the lack of a ramp would be for a tenant who uses a wheelchair.

To ensure a good fit between autistic people and housing self-determination, provision of choice, support for and assistance with individualised adaptions, affordability, and support for community inclusion are essential. These principles should guide decision-makers, planners and support providers when evaluating existing housing choices or commissioning housing.

Self-determination should be supported via robust person-centred planning, including communication support, such as using photos or symbols, for people who struggle with verbal communication.

Design and location factors

For autistic people, sensory-perceptual differences can create challenges in spaces designed for neurotypical people. These differences are individual: many prefer a low-stimulus environment, some may need or can tolerate a more stimulating environment. There is no substitute for high-quality person-centred planning to gain understanding of needs and preferences.

Recent research pinpoints additional factors that may be helpful, including individual control and input, availability of adequate support, separate spaces for different activities, access to nature, and proximity to public transport, essential services, and key social contacts (van der Veeken & van Rengs, 2012). Although several guides to designing or choosing housing for autistic people are available (e.g. Ahrendsen & Steele, 2009; 2015; Autism Speaks, 2011; Beaver, 2011; Brand, 2010; Resnick & Blackbourn, 2009), Selcer *et al* (2015) stress the crucial role of individual voice and choice. Kinnear *et al* (2015) note that evaluating 'fit' after rehousing is also critical, because unexpected or new problems may emerge.

In addition, most guidelines are written with new-build residential facilities in mind rather than adaptation of existing housing units, even though retrofitting is more likely to keep families and individuals in their existing community, and has a considerably lower cost. Adaptive applied design solutions, such as portable soundproofing features, are needed to make existing housing suitable or to adapt it to fit lifecourse changes. Very little guidance is available, other than the work of Brand and Gaudion (2012) and Lowe *et al* (2014). Solutions that are portable, adjustable, and owned by the individual are best, as these permit autistic people to bring accommodations with them when rehoused.

Of course, Universal Design (UD) principles build in flexibility for new and changing uses, and should be part of any designer's toolkit (Milton *et al*, 2016). The Design for the Mind workgroup at the Centre for Accessible Environments has been working to extend existing UD concepts to reflect neurological differences (Maslin, 2012).

Finally, it is important to consider life course changes when designing housing. Studio and one-bedroom units are certainly needed, but autistic people may have partners and/or children. Mobility limitations or additional disabilities may be present now or in the future. However, new complexes are often designed based on incorrect assumptions about the lives of people with autism. For example, research on small, parent-initiated supported housing projects for people with intellectual disabilities and/or autism in the Netherlands found that only one would accept a resident with a partner, none realised that disabled adults might have children, and most catered to 'young adults' with no provision for aging (Reindl *et al*, 2016).

Ensuring health and safety

Some housing creates increased vulnerability to crime or ill health. The author is aware of many cases where autistic adults have been placed in hostel, bed and breakfast or community housing without regard to vulnerability. Placing a person whose social understanding or communication skills are limited in close proximity to substance abusers or sexual predators seems like an obvious error, but it happens with regularity in every UK town and city.

Sometimes hard choices are made due to limited supply and high cost. When there is no alternative, commissioners and providers must do additional work to protect vulnerable tenants through enhanced security and communication features, safety training, and personnel. Neglecting this responsibility invites abuse.

Housing also needs to be regularly inspected for health and safety issues, such as rising damp and mould, electrical and gas hazards, and fall or break-in risks. Some autistic tenants need regularly scheduled welfare checks to ensure their health and safety.

Minimising intrusive support or surveillance

Individuals with moderate to severe intellectual difficulties in addition to autism can have difficulty gaining independent living skills (Matson *et al*, 2009). Appropriate support helps to overcome these barriers (Felce *et al*, 2011). Receiving support is not always a positive experience for autistic people, however, especially if staff change frequently, lack understanding, or do not know how to communicate with the person they care for.

Sensitive design can minimise the need for support with activities of daily living. For example, well-designed and clearly marked areas for grooming, dressing, clothes storage, laundry and cooking can minimise unwanted 'help'. Visual communication systems, such as colour-coding and clear instructions using words, photos or symbols, can help people with executive function or communication difficulties gain greater independence. Minimising sensory overload increases personal comfort, making staff intrusion to manage challenging behaviour less likely.

Maximising family and community inclusion

Often social housing, supported housing and residential care facilities are considered with more regard to cost than resident preference. This can result in autistic people being faced with a choice between having somewhere to live and maintaining relationships with family, friends and supporters.

The solution is for local authorities to learn about the housing needs and preferences of autistic adults and families with autistic children, and retrofit or commission adequate provision where it is actually wanted and needed. When disabled people are moved frequently or placed in unfamiliar facilities far from home, relationships can be destroyed, and vulnerability to abuse and neglect is heightened. Individualised solutions, such as extra soundproofing, blackout curtains, high-security locks, or domotics (home automation) do not need to be costly.

Some families and adults need support services to enable community inclusion. Examples include help to deal with abusive or annoying neighbours, or signposting to community services and activities.

Maximising personal choice and autonomy

An American report on the experiences of adults with autism and/or intellectual disabilities highlighted their experiences of 'community-based' facilities that are segregated, isolated, and sometimes locked. Residents' movements, communications and relationships are monitored and controlled; and choices about food, sexuality, and daily activities are limited (Barrows *et al*, 2012). These authors add that service providers have become adept at using the language of 'choice' and 'self-direction,' even as they restrict it. They state:

> 'The goal of support and services should be to maximize our independence and empowerment. Respect the dignity of risk – avoid making suggestions that could take control of us in the context of providing support … In genuine community people have names not labels, live in neighborhoods not on campuses, make their own choices, and enjoy privacy and genuine relationships of equality.'

(Barrows *et al*, 2012, p17–18)

These findings are a wake-up call for residential care providers and housing commissioners. Today, adults with disabilities, including those on the autism spectrum, expect to have a voice in decisions about their lives, including where, how and with whom they will live.

Conclusion

For everyone involved in policies or decisions about housing that impact autistic people, person-centred planning, maximising choice and autonomy, and independent living should be primary goals. An example of well-thought-through policymaking and guidance that upholds these principles has been provided by the Working Group on Autistic Spectrum Disorder (2010) regarding social housing tenancies in the Glasgow area. This document enshrines supporting choice and problem-solving as the centre of housing planning, considers what kind of tenant support might be needed for inclusion and safety, and assumes that autistic children and adults will be included in the community as a matter of course.

Indeed, addressing barriers to inclusion begins with presence in the community via housing. This is a matter not just for design and planning, but requires attention to the impact of (low) income and the availability of support for independent living.

References

Ahrentsen S & Steele K (2009) *Advancing Full Spectrum Housing for Adults with Autism Spectrum Disorders* [online]. Phoenix: Arizona Board of Regents. Available at: stardust.asu.edu/docs/stardust/advancing-full-spectrum-housing/full-report.pdf (accessed September 2017).

Autism Speaks (2011) *Housing and Residential Supports Toolkit* [online]. New York: Autism Speaks. Available at: www.autismspeaks.org/sites/default/files/housing_tool_kit_web2.pdf (accessed September 2017).

BACCH & BACD (2014/15) *Impact of Austerity Measures on Families with Disabled Children: Survey of BACCH and BACD members and child development team leads* [online]. London: British Association for Childhood Community Health and British Academy of Childhood Disability. Available at: www.bacdis.org.uk/policy/documents/ImpactofAusterityMeasuresonfamilieswithDisabledChildren16Jan2015.pdf (accessed September 2017).

Barrows M, Braddock, G, Durbin-Westby PC, Kirk S, Lakin C, Milbern S, Ne'Eman A, Robertson SM, Thayler N, Topper K, Valnes B, Ward N & Williams B (2012) *Keeping the Promise: Self advocates defining the meaning of community living* [online]. Washington, DC: Autistic Self-Advocacy Network/Self-Advocates Becoming Empowered/National Youth Leadership Network. Available at: autisticadvocacy.org/wp-content/uploads/2012/02/KeepingthePromise-SelfAdvocatesDefiningtheMeaningofCommunity.pdf (accessed September 2017).

Beaver C (2011) Designing environments for children and adults on the autism spectrum. *Good Autism Practice* **12** (1) 7–11.

Begeer S, Wierda M & Venderbosch S (2013) *Allemaal Autisme, Allemaal Anders*. De Bilt: Nederlandse Vereniging voor Autisme.

Brand A (2010) *Living in the Community: Housing design for adults with autism*. Reading: Kingwood Trust/Helen Hamlyn Centre for Design.

Brand A & Gaudion K (2012) *Exploring Sensory Preferences: Living environments for adults with autism*. Reading: Kingwood Trust/Helen Hamlyn Centre for Design.

Committee on the Rights of Persons with Disabilities (2016) *Report of the Inquiry Regarding the United Kingdom of Great Britain and Northern Ireland* [online]. Geneva: Office of the United Nations High Commissioner for Human Rights. Available at: www.ohchr.org/Documents/HRBodies/CRPD/CRPD.C.15.R.2.Rev.1-ENG.doc (accessed September 2017).

Dykens EM, Fisher MH, Taylor JL, Lambert W & Miodrag N (2014) Reducing distress in mothers of children with autism and other disabilities: a randomized trial. *Pediatrics* **134** (2) e454–e463.

Felce D, Perry J, Lowe K & Jones E (2011) The impact of autism or severe challenging behavior on lifestyle outcome in community housing. *Journal of Applied Research in Intellectual Disabilities* **24** 95–104.

Harker M & King N (2004) *Tomorrow's Big Problem: Housing options for people with autism*. London: Housing Options/National Autistic Society.

Hauben H, Coucheir M, Spooren J, McAnaney D & Delfosse C (2012) *Assessing the Impact of European Governments' Austerity Plans on the Rights of People with Disabilities* [online]. Brussels: European Foundation Centre. Available at: www.enil.eu/wp-content/uploads/2012/12/Austerity-European-Report_FINAL.pdf (accessed September 2017)

Johns N & Cooper A with Bicknell A, Batten A, Povey C, Rosenblaat M, Quinton A & Ayris E (2007) *Autism and Independence*. London: National Autistic Society.

Kinnaer M, Baumers S & Heylighen A (2015) Autism-friendly housing from the outside in and the inside out: an explorative study based on the autobiographies of autistic people. *Journal of Housing and the Built Environment* **31** (2) 179–195.

Maslin S (2012) Design for the mind: Neurodiversity and the built environment. *Access by Design* **132** 14–20.

Lowe C, Gaudion K, McGinley C & Kew A (2014) Designing living environments with adults with autism. *Tizard Learning Disability Review* **19** (2) 63–72.

Matson JL, Dempsey T & Fodstad J (2009) The effect of autism spectrum disorders on adaptive independent living skills in adults with severe intellectual disability. *Research in Developmental Disabilities* **30** (6) 1203–1211.

Milton D, Martin M & Melham P (2016) Beyond reasonable adjustment: autistic-friendly spaces and Universal Design. In: D Milton and N Martin (Eds) *Autism and Intellectual Disabilities in Adults, Vol* (pp81–86). Hove: Pavilion: Publishing and Media Ltd.

PAS (2014) *Autisme Vriendelijk Wonen*. te Nieuwegein: Vereniging Personen uit het Autisme Spectrum.

Pearson CL, Locke G, Montgomery AN & Buron L (2007) *The Applicability of Housing First Models to Homeless Persons with Serious Mental Illness* [online]. Washington DC: US Department of Housing and Urban Development. Available at: www.huduser.gov/portal/publications/homeless/hsgfirst.html (accessed September 2017).

Piazza VE, Floyd FJ, Mailick MR & Greenberg JS (2014) Coping and psychological health of aging parents of adult children with developmental disabilities. *American Journal on Intellectual and Developmental Disabilities* **119** (2) 186–198.

Reindl M-S, Waltz M & Schippers A (2016) Personalisation, self-advocacy and inclusion: an evaluation of parent-initiated supported living schemes for people with intellectual and developmental disabilities in the Netherlands. *Journal of Intellectual Disabilities* **20** (2) 121–136.

Resnick DD & Blackbourn J (2009) *Opening Doors: A discussion of residential options for adults living with autism and related disorders* [online]. Phoenix: Arizona Board of Regents. Available at: www.autismcenter.org/sites/default/files/files/openingdoors_print_042610_001.pdf (accessed September 2017).

Robertson J, Emerson E, Hattion C & Walsh PN (2001) Environmental opportunities and supports for exercising self-determination in community-based residential settings. *Research in Developmental Disabilities* **22** (6) 487–502.

Selcer A, Karlsen M, Mitchell J, Decker PJ & Durand R (2015) What do adults with ASD desire in their residence? *Housing, Care & Support* **18** (1) 31–40.

Stancliffe RJ (2001) Living with support in the community: predictors of choice and self-determination. *Mental Retardation and Developmental Disabilities Research Reviews* **7** (2) 91–98.

United Nations High Commissioner for Human Rights (2014) *Human Rights Fact Sheet 21: The right to adequate housing*. Geneva: Office of the United Nations High Commissioner for Human Rights.

Van der Veeken DR & van Rengs F (2012) *Onderzoeksverslag Woonwensen van Mensen met een Autismespectrumstoornis* [online]. Nijmegen: Hogeschool van Arnhem en Nijmegen. Available at: www.han.nl/onderzoek/kennismaken/han-sociaal/lectoraat/levensloopbegeleiding-bij-autisme/publicaties/_attachments/woonwensen_van_mensen_met_ass_autisme_2013.pdf (accessed September 2017).

Working Group on Autism Spectrum Disorder (2010) *A Practical Guide for Registered Social Landlords: Housing and Autism Spectrum Disorder* (ASD) [online]. Glasgow: Glasgow City Council. Available at: onlineborders.org.uk/sites/default/files/asdborders/files/PracticalGuideforRSLsHousingASDmarch10.pdf (accessed September 2017).

Safeguarding autistic adults in England

Dr Yo Dunn

Abstract

Adult safeguarding processes are a priority focus for adult social care, but safeguarding work with autistic adults often lacks an autism-specific focus. In this chapter I describe and analyse the vulnerabilities and strengths of autistic adults encountering various types of abuse and neglect, including:

→ Physical abuse
→ Domestic violence
→ Sexual abuse
→ Psychological abuse
→ Financial abuse
→ Modern slavery
→ Discriminatory abuse
→ Organisational abuse
→ Neglect, including self-neglect

In doing so, I argue that effective safeguarding requires practitioners to work with autistic adults to promote autonomy and support us to keep ourselves safe.

How big is the risk?

Victimisation

Safeguarding of vulnerable adults is a priority focus throughout adult social care and related services. Due to the inconsistent collection of data on autism in the UK, it is not possible to measure the proportions of autistic adults amongst those involved in safeguarding enquiries, but it will be clear to practitioners that the numbers are substantial.

People with disabilities are at greater risk of abuse than non-disabled people. At particular risk are those with speech and language difficulties (3 times greater risk), intellectual disability (4 times greater risk) and behavioural difficulties (5 times greater risk) (Sullivan & Knutson, 2000). Given that most autistic people have difficulties that may fall within one or more of these groups, it is clear that autistic people are at heightened risk of victimisation. In self-report surveys, autistic adults report high levels of victimisation, particularly 'hate crime' (bullying, verbal abuse, name calling, assaults) and 'mate crime' (being exploited or taken advantage of by someone purporting to be a friend, examples include being coerced into illegal activity, financially or sexually exploited)[1].

Abuse or neglect of autistic people is never acceptable and these substantially inflated rates of victimisation should never be considered inevitable. However, it is important to be aware of factors that may increase the vulnerability of autistic people to abuse and obstruct access to support and protection. Autistic people may:

→ tend to take what people say literally and assume they are telling the truth

→ not recognise and avoid 'high-risk' situations (such as walking alone late at night in a 'bad' part of town)

→ not recognise subtle indicators of deception or risk in other people's speech, body language or facial expression

→ have limited social networks leading to a lack of trusted people to turn to for help

→ fear being labelled as the perpetrator rather than the victim (unfortunately this is a real risk due to public perceptions of autism)

→ experience communication difficulties in trying to report abuse or seek help

→ not have been taught the vocabulary to describe inappropriate touching or other abuse

→ be wrongly assumed on the basis of intellectual ability to be able to effectively protect themselves[2]

→ have good 'book knowledge' but not be streetwise

→ be wrongly assumed (on the basis of being autistic) to be unable to give evidence or be a reliable witness[3]

→ need support in daily life (formal and/or informal), leading to relationships with unequal power balance

→ lack awareness of social 'norms' and struggle to identify behaviour as abusive or neglectful

→ have disclosures dismissed or overlooked because of a prior pattern of vexatious and/or trivial complaints and/or supplying far too much irrelevant detail.

---

1 One survey found 80% of autistic people over 16 felt bullied or taken advantage of by someone they thought was a friend: http://www.autismtogether.co.uk/wp-content/uploads/2015/07/WAS-mate-crime-report-June-2015.pdf
2 The Care Act (2014) s.42 requires local authorities to carry out an adult safeguarding enquiry only where the adult is unable to protect himself or herself against the abuse or neglect or the risk of it.
3 The use of registered intermediaries to facilitate the communication of vulnerable victims and witnesses in the criminal justice system is slowly growing and should help to reduce this.

Perpetrators

Autistic adults are far more likely to be victims than perpetrators. Generally, autistic people are particularly likely to follow rules and laws rigidly. Most autistic people have high moral standards and are extremely law-abiding. However, it is also true that autistic adults can behave in challenging or problematic ways and these can sometimes result in autistic people coming into contact with the criminal justice system. 16% of people placed in custody meet one or more of the assessment criteria for mental disorder (Maguire, 2010) and 'a consensus figure of 50-60% of young people who are involved in offending having speech, language and communication needs is emerging' (Gregory & Bryan, 2011).

It is possible to describe some loose categories for potentially offending behaviours of autistic individuals:

- → Innocent behaviour being misinterpreted (including 'social error' offences).
- → Distress and/or 'challenging behaviour'.
- → Not knowing something was wrong/illegal.
- → Being exploited/manipulated.
- → Obsessions and rigidity (including in arguments).
- → Offending behaviour for non-autism related reasons (just like anyone else).

(Gwilliam, 2009)

Types of abuse

Physical abuse

Autistic people may be at risk of physical assault both by family/carers and by strangers. The communication difficulties, conflicting needs and stress which can arise within families can be particularly acute in families which include an autistic person, and this can increase the risks. Autistic people are at particular risk of being assaulted by strangers because our unusual behaviours or ways of moving may attract adverse attention or because social errors or miscommunications can trigger a violent response. Autistic people of all ages experience bullying to such an extent that we may consider it 'normal'. In care environments, particularly those where autistic needs are not well understood or which subject autistic people to high level of environmental or other stress, autistic people may behave in ways which challenge care staff and other residents. This puts them at risk of abusive responses including physical restraint, seclusion and the misuse of sedating medications.

Autistic adults may occasionally perpetrate violence and may be particularly vulnerable to inadvertently perpetrating threatening behaviour. Particularly when distressed, autistic people may speak at a high volume, use language, gestures or otherwise behave in ways which are unacceptable to other people (such as encroaching on the personal space of others). These behaviours may be perceived as threatening or aggressive. The autistic person may or may not (no matter how 'intelligent') be aware at the time of how their behaviour is being perceived by others and may fail to anticipate such reactions.

Domestic violence

As mentioned previously, autistic people may experience abuse from parents and other family members. However autistic people are also particularly vulnerable to domestic violence from partners. Contrary to popular myth, autistic people are capable of forming close emotional bonds with others and autistic teenagers and adults can and do form heathy intimate relationships. However, autistic teenagers and adults may also struggle to identify patterns of behaviour towards them from a partner which are 'abnormal' or 'unhealthy' and may lack the social networks to have any basis for comparison. Most autistic people are accustomed to receiving negative reactions from other people in social relationships and to being told or believing that they are the person at fault. Most autistic people also have less knowledge and awareness of social 'norms' than neurotypical peers. So, autistic teenagers and adults are particularly vulnerable to believing that they must be the one at fault and failing to recognise behaviour from a partner as exploitative, manipulative, unhealthy or abusive.

Autistic people may also be at risk of perpetrating harassment, stalking or similar behaviours. Issues in this area can arise from a combination of obsessive tendencies and potentially poor understanding of how social interactions may be perceived or experienced by others.

> **Case example**
>
> Jordan (19 years old) is in his first year at university. He has spent some weeks plucking up the courage to ask a young woman on his course (Laura) out for coffee. When he finally manages to ask her, she politely declines saying that she is too busy. Disappointed but determined to solve the problem, Jordan uses the web and social media to research Laura's timetable, find out what social and leisure activities she attends and which buses she takes to travel to university. In an effort to be helpful, he sends Laura a series of lengthy emails explaining several different ways in which she could make time in her schedule to have coffee with him.

Sexual abuse

Sexuality, in the context of modern life in the UK, is an area of human interaction which involves complex and constantly evolving social rules and norms. Social communication about sex is rarely clear, literal and explicit. Much is implied or inferred and innuendo is commonplace. This communicative and social environment is very confusing from an autistic point of view.

Recent years have seen increasing awareness of and public discussion of child sexual abuse and exploitation. However, the high levels of victimisation amongst disabled children and adults are less visible. Increasing awareness is to be welcomed and it has led to a flurry of new sexual offences including some focused specifically on protection of people with 'mental disorders'[4] (a legal term which includes autism). Politically popular as introducing new offences may be, the evidence-base is quite clear that good quality relationship and sex education is far more effective in actually reducing rates of victimisation (Finkelhor, 2009).

Specialist sex and relationship education, specifically for autistic children, teenagers and adults is essential to improve safeguarding in this area. This is because autistic people (including those who do not have an intellectual disability) often need more explicit and literal teaching than may be considered appropriate for a general audience, and it is

---

4 See Sexual Offences Act (2003) s.30-44.

particularly important that sex and relationships education is embedded within wider teaching and support with social relationships (Hartman, 2014). Unfortunately, provision is limited and patchy. The needs of autistic children in mainstream schools and autistic young adults beyond school age are often overlooked. Autism is a developmental disorder and it is common in the autistic community for young adults to mature over a longer period of time than neurotypical peers. So autistic young adults in their late teens and into their 20s and beyond may be continuing to develop and explore their sexuality. They may have further questions and need additional levels of knowledge at this point that they were not ready or able to take in at a younger age.

The massive impact of technology on social norms, including sexual relationships, has both positive and negative results for autistic people.

Positive	Negative
Increased accessibility of information.	Highly variable quality of information.
Easy access to a much wider social group, including niche and non-mainstream identities and interests.	Social interaction can extend into private spaces 24 hours a day, including bullying, victimisation and exploitation.
Peer support for those who identify as LGBTQI.	Easy to inadvertently cross social or legal boundaries.

On the positive side, information about every conceivable subject is now available through mediums which autistic people often find more accessible and without requiring human interaction. The growth of online dating and social media have provided new opportunities and ways of developing relationships which can have significant advantages for autistic people. Autistic people often have interests, traits and identities which are less 'mainstream'. Common interests in the autistic community include (amongst many, many others) trains and transport; role-playing and trading card games; Star Trek and other 'cult' tv series; maths, computing and physics. Although reliable statistical data is difficult to come by, it appears to be the case that autistic people are more likely to identify as questioning their gender, trans or non-binary[5]. There may also be a somewhat higher proportion of autistic people who are (or at least who publicly identify as) gay or bisexual than the proportions found in a neurotypical population. The accessibility of a much larger range of individuals online compared to those in an autistic person's immediate physical community offers valuable opportunities to form social relationships with peers with similar characteristics, identities, interests or traits.

On the negative side, the quality of information available online is highly variable. Autistic people are vulnerable to scams and exploitation (including sexual exploitation) online. There are particular risks around being pressured or manipulated into transmitting explicit 'selfies' and then becoming vulnerable to blackmail and 'revenge porn'. Social (and sexual) interaction extends into what were formerly private spaces 24 hours a day and this can include bullying, victimisation and exploitation.

Autistic people are highly unlikely to be sexual predators or pose any sort of risk to others. However, some autistic people may be at risk of perpetrating particular kinds of sexual offending. Lack of knowledge and the complexity of the social rules in this area of human interaction can result in some autistic adults seeking to meet their sexual needs in ways which contravene the law and/or infringe on the rights of others, usually without deliberately intending to do so. Nick Dubin, an autistic self-advocate living in the US, has bravely written about his experience of being convicted of accessing child pornography following naïve exploration of his emerging sexuality in his early 20s.

'Like many people with Asperger's who have little social contact, my computer was my major link to the outside world. I relied heavily on it to gather research for my studies, to obtain information about my special interests, and as a way to connect with others. For example, I would spend hours every day on the internet finding jazz music and then I would post all my recommendations on Facebook.

At the time it seemed like a natural progression for me to go from looking at pornographic magazines to viewing the same type of material on the computer. Using the computer was certainty a more comfortable and safer way to explore my sexuality than dating, travelling to Nevada, or going to adult bookstores.'

(Dubin, 2014, p.98)

He explains that his psychological and sexual development was (as is typical of autistic people) substantially at odds with his intellectual development and his chronological age. Whilst in no way condoning or seeking to justify the viewing of child pornography, he painstakingly sets out how he felt internally like a young adolescent and sought images of those he saw as his 'peers', without, at the time, realising that those children had been victimised in the making of the images or even that his actions were illegal. Following his conviction he became aware that he was not the only autistic young adult to have made a similar, catastrophic mistake. He concludes that many autistic people 'simply have a different psychosexual development from their neurotypical counterparts and this difference can sometimes affect interpersonal relationships and encounters with strangers, as well as sexual exploration that can take place on the computer'. A great deal can be done to mitigate the risk of autistic people becoming either victims or perpetrators of sexual abuse through providing good quality and autism-specific education from an early age, and continuing access to such education throughout transitions and life stages (including in adult life).

Psychological abuse

Psychological abuse is a particularly problematic area for autistic people. Autistic people may experience interactions as distressing which the person do not intend to be abuse. So it is particularly important in this area to recognise that unintentional abuse is still abuse, and not dismiss an autistic person's experience merely because a neurotypical person might not experience the same behaviour as abusive.

---

5 A recent review of available clinical and empirical data by van der Miesen et al (2016) found that gender dysphoria and ASD co-occur frequently, although, as yet, there is insufficient evidence to support any of the varied hypotheses on potential reasons for this.

Case example

A neurotypical counsellor assures Issac that his conversations with her are confidential. After the counselling sessions have finished, Issac receives a copy of the report which his counsellor has sent to his GP summarising the outcome of their sessions. She considers this an entirely normal action. To her it is just a summary and does not contain the types of details she would consider confidential. From Issac's point of view, however, the assurance of confidentiality was an absolute. The counsellor had not drawn his attention to her mention of feedback to his GP during their discussion about confidentiality. So Issac experiences this as a betrayal of trust and feels angry. On a future occasion, he refuses an offer of counselling saying that he can't trust counsellors.

A typical example is the concept of 'teasing', which is often experienced by autistic people as distressing because it can be very difficult to determine whether a comment is intended to be taken literally. Repeated 'teasing' of an autistic person who is distressed by it, is a common form of bullying.

Another example is the issue of honesty. Autistic perceptions of honesty tend to be much more black and white than neurotypical perceptions. Consequently an autistic person may consider all statements which are not literally true to be lies. This lack of mutual understanding between autistic people and neurotypical professionals can result in behaviour which the neurotypical professional considers entirely normal being experienced as a violation of trust by the autistic person.

Blaming and controlling behaviours towards autistic people are particularly common. More verbal autistic people are frequently blamed for social errors which are a result of being autistic – because others (often unthinkingly) assume that someone who is intellectually able should 'know better'. Controlling behaviours are often excused towards autistic people as resulting from an autistic person's 'challenging' behaviour (i.e. victim blaming). These include inappropriate and unnecessary restraint (including inappropriate use of medication), unnecessarily rigid and inappropriate policies and procedures.

Controlling and paternalistic behaviours towards autistic people are also often excused as being 'in their best interests'. Disabled adults are frequently treated in ways which are inappropriate for their chronological age and paternalistic cultures remain deeply embedded and widespread within special schooling, adult care environments and in healthcare.

Another common experience for autistic people is that of being isolated and excluded from social groups. This can easily occur inadvertently as a result of misunderstandings (such as an assumption that an autistic person does not wish to interact) or uncertainty as to how to facilitate the inclusion of an autistic person. However, exclusion from social groups can readily become a persistent experience for autistic people and, when the exclusion is involuntary and unwelcome can be abusive. Effective strategies for making social environments 'autistic friendly' include:

- clear, consistent and detailed information about times, locations and expectations
- time to adjust to new environments and to process information or questions
- absence of direct pressure to interact (e.g. being asked a direct question in front of an audience)
- facilitated opportunities for interaction (e.g. being part of a small group to whom questions are generally directed where it is clear that anyone is free to respond; being 'introduced' to people)
- if possible, a quiet, interaction-free space to retreat to
- tolerance and forgiveness of social 'errors'.

Financial or material abuse

Financial abuse occurs in a variety of situations and forms. So-called 'mate' crime; exploitation by those who claim to be friends, is a form of abuse which autistic people are particularly likely to experience. One survey found that 80% of autistic people over the age of 16 report having been a victim of mate crime (Wirral Autistic Society, 2015). It can be very difficult for autistic people to distinguish between stated intent and actual intent. In other words, autistic people are generally very trusting and tend to believe what people say. This can increase vulnerability to exploitation of all types.

Autistic adults also experience financial abuse from those in positions of trust with responsibility for supporting an individual with managing their money or financial affairs. There will always be risks of dishonesty where one person manages money for another person. However, practitioners can reduce these risks by promoting and supporting the direct involvement of autistic adults in their own financial affairs, including where the adult has an appointed deputy and/or an appointee.

Case example

Ferenc Virag, an autistic artist, lives in a specialist residential provision. He has a particular focus on light and shade and is interested in working with glass. Since at least 2004, Ferenc has been expressing his desire to have his own kiln. Ferenc is a meticulous and careful person with good fine motor control. Ferenc's friend, Dinah Murray, remarks that staff always promise to 'look into it' but nothing ever happens. On one occasion, Ferenc showed his drawing of a kiln to a member of staff. She responded by saying 'No, Ferenc! You know very well that it's too dangerous'.

Dinah arranged for Ferenc to visit a local jewellery school accompanied by his support worker and a manager. Ferenc rolled up his sleeves as soon as he realised he was being allowed to cut glass, and proceeded to cut a set of perfectly matched straight-edged rectangular small panes which stacked into a gleamingly varied transparent block. He did this with immaculate efficiency and speed. The jewellery school instructor explained the pros and cons of the two small kilns she uses. Ferenc again made it clear that he would very much like one of his own. By highlighting the importance of person-centred care and pointing to Mental Capacity Act principles, Dinah was finally able to persuade staff to support Ferenc in getting a kiln of his own.

Ferenc has finally, in 2017, been enabled to obtain a kiln, tools and materials. Ferenc was happy for me to tell the story of his long wait for a kiln and he is very much looking forward to being able to use it.

The background to Ferenc's story is told in Murray (2013).

Modern slavery

Vulnerable adults are likely in general to be at increased risk of this form of abuse and it is likely that this includes autistic adults. However, because the widespread recognition of this form of abuse is relatively new, knowledge in this area is still developing. It is likely that autistic adults may be particularly vulnerable to this type of victimisation for similar reasons to those discussed earlier.

Discriminatory abuse

Unfortunately disability discrimination remains remarkably widespread and difficult to eliminate. The Equality Act (2010) (and its forerunner the Disability Discrimination Act 1995) is a positive step, however its weakness in practice limits the practical benefit. Disability discrimination is extremely difficult to prove and day-to-day struggles to obtain the most basic adjustments and establish that they are 'reasonable' are the norm for disabled people.

Autism is an invisible disability. There is no obvious sign that someone is autistic. This has positive and negative implications in terms of discrimination. On the one hand, it is possible for some autistic people to minimise the risk of discrimination by not disclosing their disability. Many autistic people feel forced to do this at times (especially in order to access employment). However, trying to 'act the part' of a neurotypical person is usually a very demanding and stressful experience. This results in significantly increased stress for many autistic people who do this and is rarely an entirely positive experience.

Case example

Morgan (23) submitted a formal complaint to her council via their complaints process. She attached 25 documents, setting out a 2 year long history of her complaints to Horizons care agency (who provided her support workers). All of her complaints alleged discrimination and psychological abuse. She described trivial events in great detail. These included an incident on a day trip to the seaside when, she alleged, a support worker discriminated against her because she asked if she would like an ice cream, but didn't ask what flavour she wanted and returned with a vanilla cone instead of the strawberry one she would have preferred. Another complaint concerned what she described as 'bullying' by another support worker who had pushed a note under her door one evening reminding her of an appointment the next day. She viewed this as bullying because he had not knocked on her door and spoken to her in person.

The council believed that it had conscientiously considered and responded to the complaint, although it concluded that it was unfounded. The council helped Morgan to move her support to another agency (Sunshine Support).

Morgan was not satisfied with the council's response and continued to write letters to the ombudsman, the CQC and her MP about her previous allegations. Soon she made new allegations of verbal abuse and bullying about a member of staff from Sunshine Support and began to include these in her regular complaint letters.

Consider the likely outcome of investigations into Morgan's new allegations. What if a member of staff from Sunshine Support is (from an objective perspective) bullying and verbally abusing Morgan?

On the other hand, the invisibility of autism leads many autistic people to constantly have the existence, reality and severity of autistic difficulties questioned, denied or trivialised. Autistic people who use speech and do not have an intellectual disability are often assumed (even by some autism professionals) to have a 'mild' form of autism. This is a dubious assumption and for many individuals is highly unhelpful. Autistic people typically have 'spiky' profiles – they tend to have highly varying levels of ability and disability which are not particularly consistent across different skills. Therefore autistic people also experience discrimination in the form of being treated as not disabled or as 'not really' disabled.

Discrimination and discriminatory abuse are widespread and most autistic people experience them frequently. But it is also fair to say, that there are autistic people who tend to ascribe every negative experience to discrimination and struggle to recognise the difference between fair and reasonable differentiation on objective grounds (such as giving different grades to recognise different levels of academic attainment) and unreasonable discrimination on the grounds of a protected characteristic (such as disability). In combination with obsessiveness and focus on details, this common autistic difficulty can result in an autistic person failing to be heard when seeking to report actual abuse or discrimination.

Organisational abuse

When considering organisational abuse, thoughts inevitably turn to the Winterbourne View case. It is undoubtedly the case that a significant proportion of those detained in Assessment and Treatment Units and in other institutional care environments are autistic. Abusive cultures must be recognised and challenged and it is important to be aware of the potential for care environments to develop into abusive environments and develop strong approaches to prevention.

Total attachment theory suggests that abusive care environments may be more likely to develop where staff become overwhelmed by the pressures of the caring role and respond by dissociating and detaching emotionally from those who they are caring for (Harbottle *et al*, 2014). Autistic people may be particularly likely to experience organisational abuse. Autistic people can present with behaviour which poses significant challenges for staff working with them. If staff struggle to understand and relate to the likely causes of

Case example

Sisi (an autistic adult who does not speak) is rocking and staring at the floor. Ian – a care worker – comes towards Sisi, sits on the floor in front of her and says 'Hello'. Sisi jumps up, screams and pushes Ian away from her.

Ian describes the incident to his line manager: 'I tried to engage Sisi but she didn't like me saying 'Hello' to her and pushed me away. Perhaps she would engage better with a female worker?'

How might Sisi describe the encounter? Perhaps she was watching a fascinating pattern of sunlight on the floor and enjoying the sensory experience. Suddenly an object disrupted the pattern which made it 'wrong' and she needed to get her pattern back to make it 'right' again. She expressed her distress at the disruption by screaming and pushed the object out of the way of the rays of sunlight.

an autistic person's behaviour, then they can easily become overwhelmed.

Key factors of organisational abuse:

(1) Different ways of seeing the world

Autistic people see the world in a fundamentally different way to people who are not autistic. The majority of people in society (and therefore the majority of care workers) are not autistic. One understanding of some of the cognitive issues in autism suggests that autistic people tend to be strong at systemising (the drive to analyse and construct systems) whilst not being as naturally inclined towards intuitive or empathetic thinking (Baron-Cohen, 2009; De Martino *et al*, 2008). Within the care sector, on the other hand, empathetic thinking and behaviours are strongly encouraged and individuals with strong intuitive or empathetic thinking and behaviours may be more likely to be selected for care work during recruitment processes. This can result in a particularly wide gulf between an autistic person's perspective and the perspective of the care worker who is supporting them.

(2) Behaviourist approaches

Behaviourist approaches are ubiquitous within care services. Positive behaviour support (PBS) has been widely adopted and is widely trained as the 'gold standard' of support for those presenting with behaviour which challenges (many of whom will be autistic). As the National Autism Project report highlights, 'PBS is built upon theory and an evidence base that is not autism specific' (Iemmi, 2017). In theory, PBS is person-centred, includes the perspective of the autistic person and its goal is to enhance quality of life. In practice, however, PBS is all too often simply used as a label for crude behaviourist approaches which 'train' individuals to stop displaying a behaviour which is deemed 'inappropriate' by others. The functional analysis (usually using the 'ABC' approach), advocated by PBS focuses on 'triggers' of 'behaviour' and 'consequences'. This promotes a focus on containment and management of the 'behaviour' that is troubling or challenging to neurotypical staff members and their perceptions of what immediately 'set it off'.

Behaviourist approaches can form a useful part of a professional 'toolkit' and can be beneficial when used appropriately – for example to support an autistic person to manage an obsessive-compulsive behaviour which is troubling them.

However, they do not address or deal with the actual underlying causes of behaviour. When they are used inappropriately, even by well-meaning staff, they can easily become a form of organisational abuse. An autistic person may well behave in a manner which does not conform to the needs or expectations of a care environment and which challenges those around them. Underlying causes are likely to include pain, sensory distress and acute stress. 'Training' an autistic person to stop displaying their distress, whilst failing to address the environmental causes of that distress, is abusive.

(3) Poor understanding of autism even within supposedly autism specialist services

Issues (1) and (2) are worsened by the poor level of knowledge and understanding of autism amongst staff. Few staff have had access to more than basic 'awareness' training, which is wholly inadequate. Even where staff have had more advanced training, the content is often largely theoretical and lacking in practical strategies for actually working with autistic people day-to-day. Most autism training presents a rather dated model of autism in terms of differences from the neurotypical (predominantly social) 'norm' as the problem, rather than addressing causes of stress and distress for autistic people and how these can be reduced in the environment. This reinforces the perception that the goal of support for autistic people is normalisation.

Poor understanding of autism at the management level can (usually inadvertently) lead to policies and practices which are not at all autistic friendly. A common example is the prevalence of approaches to working with autistic people which impose constant activity and constant social interaction. Many autistic people need large amounts of 'down time' with low levels of activity and an absence of social interaction. This can be vital to autistic well-being. Rarely is this respected by care services where regulatory regimes, commissioning systems and management approaches all tend to operate on the unspoken assumption that imposing constant activity and social interaction on service users indicates 'good' care.

Neglect and acts of omission

One key issue for autistic people in this area is access to healthcare. The autistic population have increased health risks and reduced life expectancy at the same time as facing multiple obstacles to accessing healthcare (National Children's Group, 2016). Current pressures on local authority budgets mean that it is ever harder for autistic people to access support to: eat nutritious meals, monitor health conditions, obtain and take medication and to communicate with health professionals. NHS pressures mean that health services are more noisy, busy and chaotic than ever, and often require coping with long waits. Increasingly, healthcare resources are rationed by 'gatekeeping' procedures. The urgency and seriousness of a medical problem may be decided over the phone and depend on the patient's responses to pre-set questions. The responses given by an autistic patient may differ from the typical due to communication and sensory differences, potentially leading to unreliable conclusions about the seriousness or urgency of a health condition.

Self-neglect

In some instances, self-neglect can be a safeguarding concern[6]. Where an adult is unable to protect themselves by controlling their own behaviour, they may need external support to protect them from self-neglect. Autistic people may self-neglect in a variety of ways including:

→ poor self-care due to lack of social awareness and/or sensory factors

→ poor self-care due to inertia or catatonic symptoms

→ poor self-care due to executive function deficits (poor sequencing, organising)

→ hoarding (autistic rigidity can lead to OCD)

→ eating disorders.

Patterns of abuse

It is particularly important for autistic people that professionals

---

6 Care Act Statutory Guidance, chapter 14.

record and appropriately share information in order to identify patterns of abuse. Autistic people may have difficulties with autobiographical memory (recall of personal experiences) and may not retain all their experiences over time.

Summary and key points

→ Autistic people experience high rates of victimisation across virtually all types of abuse and neglect. Autistic people may be at increased risk due to perceptions of vulnerability, isolation and/or behaviours which do not conform to social norms.

→ 'High-functioning' autistic people are often, wrongly, assumed not to be vulnerable due to their language and intellectual skills. However, they too experience high rates of victimisation.

→ Autistic people are generally law-abiding, but may (mostly inadvertently) encounter the criminal justice system.

→ Over-protection and paternalism towards autistic adults increases vulnerability. Good quality autism-specific education around sexuality and social interaction and the promotion of autonomy reduce vulnerability.

References

Baron-Cohen S (2009) Autism: the empathizing-systematising (E-S) theory. *The Year in Cognitive Neuroscience* **1156** 68–80.

De Martino B, Harrison NA, Knafo S, Bird G, Dolan RJ (2008) Explaining enhanced logical consistency during decision making in autism. *Journal of Neuroscience* **28** (42) 10746–10750.

Dubin (2014) Doctoral degree: it was the best of times, it was the worst of times. In: T Attwood, I Henault & N Dubin (Eds) *The Autism Spectrum, Sexuality and the Law* (p98–101). London: Jessica Kingsley Publishers.

Finkelhor D (2009) The prevention of childhood sexual abuse [online]. *The Future of Children* **19** (2) 169–194. Available at: http://www.unh.edu/ccrc/pdf/CV192.pdf (accessed September 2017).

Gregory J & Bryan K (2011) Speech and language therapy intervention with a group of persistent and prolific young offenders in a non-custodial setting with previously undiagnosed speech, language and communication difficulties. *International Journal of Language and Communication Disorders* **46** (2) 202–215.

Gwilliam P (2009) *Police awareness of autism and how to deal with the criminal justice system, Autscape presentation*. Available at: http://www.autscape.org/2009/presentations#police-autism (accessed September 2017).

Harbottle H, Jones MR, Thompson LM (2014) From reactionary to activist: a model that works. *The Journal of Adult Protection* **16** (2) 113–119.

Hartman D (2014) *Sexuality and Relationship Education for Children and Adolescents with Autism Spectrum Disorders: A professional's guide to understanding, preventing issues, supporting sexuality and responding to inappropriate behaviours*. London: Jessica Kingsley Publishers.

Iemmi V, Knapp M & Ragan I (2017) *The Autism Dividend: Reaping rewards of better investment* [online]. National Autism Project. Available at: http://nationalautismproject.org.uk/wp-content/uploads/2017/01/autism-dividend-report.pdf (accessed September 2017).

Maguire M (2010) *Not a Marginal Issue: Mental health and the criminal justice system in Northern Ireland*. Northern Ireland: CJINI.

Murray D (2013) Art … a positive necessity of life. *Autonomy, The Critical Journal of Interdisciplinary Autism Studies* **1** (2).

National Children's Group (2016) *A Spectrum of Obstacles: An inquiry into access to healthcare for autistic people*. Westminster Commission on Autism.

Sullivan PM & Knutson JF (2000) Maltreatment and disabilities: a population-based epidemiological study. *Child Abuse and Neglect* **24** 1257–1273.

van der Miesen, Hurley H & de Vries AL (2016) Gender dysphoria and autism spectrum disorder: A narrative review. *International Review of Psychiatry* **28** (1) 70–80.

Wirral Autistic Society (2015) *Mate Crime in Merseyside* [online]. Available at: http://www.autismtogether.co.uk/wp-content/uploads/2015/07/WAS-mate-crime-report-June-2015.pdf (accessed September 2017).

Section 2:
Participatory research methods

A socio-legal analysis of the Mental Capacity Act (2005) and its implications for participation in autism-related research

Gillian Loomes

Abstract

The field of autism research is expanding rapidly, but surrounding this growth is a complex debate around the desired priorities for such research. This debate reflects the wider political tensions within autistic and autism communities characterised as the 'autism war'. In this chapter, it is argued that a key consideration for those concerned with autism-related research in England and Wales is the Mental Capacity Act (2005), which provides a legal framework for research production and participation involving adults who lack the capacity to provide informed consent. An overview of this legal framework is presented and the challenges and opportunities it represents for those planning and producing research on the contested 'battleground' of the 'autism war' are considered.

Introduction: autism research – changing landscape and rugged terrain

The field of autism research is growing exponentially. A significant increase in the noted prevalence of autism globally has triggered a need for better understanding and evidence-based practice to facilitate the support of autistic people in the social world (Pellicano *et al*, 2014). The response to this need has been striking, particularly in the United States (Dawson, 2013), where in 2010 alone, federal and private funding for autism research exceeded $400 million (Office of Autism Research Coordination, National Institute of Mental Health, on behalf of the Interagency Autism Coordinating Committee (IACC), 2012). Likewise, the UK experienced a significant increase in the funding allocated to autism research in the decade between 2004 and 2014 (Pellicano *et al*, 2014; Charman & Clare, 2004).

Surrounding this pattern of increased funding is a complex web of interacting, and often challenging and competing political discourses (threads of written and spoken communication and debate), concerning the desired priorities of such autism-related research. A key study by Pellicano *et al* (2014) highlighted a significant disparity between the types of research to which funding in the UK was largely allocated, and the views and priorities of autistic and autism communities[1]. Of particular note is the desire within these communities for '*… research that could help them, their families or those they work with in the here-and-now*' (Pellicano *et al*, 2014: p768), and '*… those areas of research that have the greatest hope of enhancing the life chances of autistic people and their families*' such as those that may lead to more employment opportunities and social connections, and an increase in the mental health and material well-being of autistic people (Pellicano *et al*, 2014, p766). This is in stark contrast to the funding priorities of government and non-government organisations over the past two decades, analysis of which shows that the majority of funded projects focus on 'basic science'; neural and cognitive systems, genetics and other risk factors (Charman & Clare, 2004; Krahn & Fenton, 2012; Office of Autism Research Coordination, National Institute of Mental Health, on behalf of the IACC, 2012; Singh *et al*, 2009).

Despite such funding trends favouring and prioritising 'basic science', the 'real-world' focus that is desired by autism (and arguably especially autistic) communities, is apparent in the emergence of autism-related social research, including research framed in resistance to what is often perceived as the socially oppressive nature of psychological theorising in relation to autism. For example Melanie Yergeau's essay,

---

[1] The phrase 'autistic and autism communities' is used to denote the distinct but overlapping social and cultural groupings of autistic people themselves and the families, paid and unpaid supporters and other 'stakeholders' who are concerned with autism-related practice.

an 'autie-ethnographic narrative traces the problems with and limits of theory of mind (ToM)' (Yergeau, 2013). This emerging sub-field of autism research may also be considered alongside a commitment to greater involvement and participation on the part of autistic people themselves in autism research – examples of which are apparent in the ESRC-funded seminar series on *Shaping Autism Research in the UK* (Shaping Autism Research in the UK, 2015), and in the work of the Participatory Autism Research Collective (PARC), a 'community for people who want to promote autistic involvement in autistic research' in order:

> '… to bring autistic people, including scholars and activists, together with early career researchers who work with autistic people … to build a community network where those who wish to see more significant involvement of autistic people in autism research can share knowledge and expertise.'

(Participatory Autism Research Collective, 2017)

It is clear then that the landscape of autism research is complex, with often competing agendas between those who advocate a 'basic-science' approach to identifying the underlying biological, neurological causes of autism and associated 'risk factors,' and those who seek an approach, often grounded in qualitative social research methodologies, which aims to contribute to the understanding of autism as it is experienced in the social world, and thereby to improve the lives of autistic people 'in the here and now'. It is also apparent that participation in, and direction of, the agendas of autism-related research are key emerging discourses, particularly among autistic people themselves.

It should also be said though, that such research-focused debates do not occur in a vacuum. Rather, that the complexities in prioritisation of autism-related research agendas both represent and reproduce the politics and 'real-world' social functioning of the autistic and autism communities outside of the direct sphere of research. Research priorities are a core part of a much wider political landscape of competing agendas surrounding autism, which clearly forms 'more than an abstract topic for academic discussion' (Pitney, 2015, p2). The psychological, social and economic stakes surrounding such agendas are high, and beliefs and concerns are often deeply held and passionately defended. Indeed, in describing what he refers to as 'the autism war', Professor Nick Hodge outlines the existence of two camps among autism stakeholders – one of which 'sees autism as a tragedy' and campaigns 'to raise money to find the cause and then a cure' for autism, with the other arguing that 'autism is a culture that needs to be enabled' and advocating the use of funding 'to support people with autism and their families' (Hodge, 2017).

The tension between these two competing agendas is palpable, and is further illustrated by Pitney (2015) who refers to the fraught discourse between what he also refers to as two camps (Pitney, 2015, p43). He quotes the autistic self-advocate, Michael John Carley, founder of the Global and Regional Asperger Syndrome Partnership, who points to the emotional harm experienced by many autistic people who 'grow up having to hear words like "cure", "disease", "defeat" and "combat"' in relation to their autistic identity' (Pitney, 2015, p43). He then contrasts this with reference to the views held by some parents of autistic people, who point to the diversity and range of abilities among the autistic population, summarising this view as:

> '*It is one thing to say that autism is just a "difference" when it involves a high-functioning person with a college degree. It is another when the person is nonverbal or lacks bowel control.*'

(Pitney, 2015: 43)

Here then, we see highlighted a key element of the discourse underpinning the political tensions that are produced and enacted in the autistic and autism communities, particularly regarding funding and research priorities – that of the heterogeneity of the autistic population. As Pitney suggests, the fact that the autistic population (in common with the non-autistic population) includes individuals with intellectual disability who may not communicate verbally, alongside those perceived to be of greater cognitive (and particularly verbal and vocal) abilities, is central to many claims concerning prioritisation and representation in autism-related research agendas.

In this sense, the field of autism research presents a microcosm of wider concerns that have been voiced within the sphere of disability activism surrounding the right to active participation by disabled people in academic research, as well as to have control over the design of such research (Barnes, 1996; Oliver, 1992), and the risk of silencing disabled 'voices' through exclusion from research (Oliver, 1993; Nind & Searle, 2009). However, while such concerns have been framed as a discourse between the disabled and non-disabled communities, with the oppressive and emancipatory scope of research being considered in relation to the disabled community, it seems that the heterogeneous nature of the autistic population, particularly in relation to perceived cognitive and verbal abilities, crystallises such discourses within the autistic and autism communities themselves.

Consequently, a consideration at the heart of the complexity of the political landscape surrounding autism research, and underpinning the concerns of some stakeholders, particularly the parents and carers referenced by Pitney (2015) is the issue of participation and representation in research of autistic adults with co-morbid intellectual disability, who lack the mental capacity to provide informed consent to such participation. In England and Wales, the legal framework governing such questions of participation is set out in the Mental Capacity Act (2005), and it is with the implications of this legal framework for the developing discourses surrounding autism research that the remainder of this article is concerned.

The Mental Capacity Act (2005): an overview

The Mental Capacity Act (2005) (MCA) is a ground-breaking piece of legislation in force in England and Wales. It applies to individuals over the age of 16, and is underpinned by five key principles, which apply 'for the purposes of this Act' (MCA, s1(1)). These principles are as follows:

→ A person must be assumed to have capacity unless it is established that he lacks capacity (MCA, s1(2)).

→ A person is not to be treated as unable to make a decision unless all practicable steps to help him to do so have been taken without success (MCA, s1(3)).

→ A person is not to be treated as unable to make a decision merely because he makes an unwise decision (MCA, s1(4)).

→ An act done, or decision made, under this Act for, or on behalf of a person who lacks capacity must be done, or made in his best interests (MCA, s1(5)).

→ Before the act is done, or the decision is made, consideration must be given to whether the purpose for which it is needed can be as effectively achieved in a way that is less restrictive of the person's rights and freedom of action (MCA, s1(5)).

The MCA sets out a framework for the assessment of mental capacity in relation to specific decisions, and for making decisions in the 'best interests' of those individuals deemed to lack capacity. This assessment framework involves a 2-stage test for the assessment of mental capacity. Firstly, a diagnostic element:

> 'A person lacks capacity in relation to a matter if at the material time he is unable to make a decision for himself in relation to a matter because of an impairment of, or disturbance in the functioning of, the mind or brain.'

(MCA, s2(1))

Secondly, a functional description of the four elements of decision-making required for mental capacity in respect of the specific decision in question to be established. These involve the ability to:

a. Understand the information relevant to the decision.
b. Retain that information.
c. Use or weigh that information as part of the process of making a decision.
d. Communicate the decision (whether by talking, using sign language or by any other means).

Therefore, if it is ascertained that the individual is experiencing 'an impairment of, or disturbance in the functioning of the mind or brain' and that they are unable to demonstrate the ability to fulfil any one of the four elements of the functional test, they will be deemed to lack capacity in relation to the specific decision at issue. It is estimated that at any time approximately two million people in England and Wales will lack the capacity to make decisions for themselves, and that they are cared for by approximately six million paid or unpaid carers (Social Care Institute for Excellence, 2016), making the reach of the MCA extensive.

Where an individual is deemed to lack capacity, the MCA sets out, in the absence of a valid and applicable advance decision from a person who had capacity at that time, how the decision should be made in the individual's 'best interests'. This is detailed in section 4 of the MCA. In particular, those making decisions on behalf of individuals lacking capacity must take into account:

→ 'the person's past and present wishes and feelings (and in particular, any relevant written statement made by him when he had capacity' (MCA, s4(6)(a))

→ 'the beliefs and values that would be likely to influence his decision if he had capacity' (MCA, s4(6)(b))

→ 'the other factors that he would be likely to consider if he were able to do so' (s4(6)(c) MCA 2005).

Therefore, unlike in some other jurisdictions, the approach set out in the MCA does not represent an attempt at 'substituted judgment' (where the decision-maker seeks to make the decision the individual lacking capacity themselves would have made). However, recent case-law, including notably the case of Briggs v Briggs,[2] which was concerned with the withdrawal of life-sustaining treatment from an individual in a minimally conscious state (MCS) has emphasised the centrality of a person's own (prior) wishes, feelings, beliefs and values in the making of best interest decisions.

The MCA, along with the related code of practice and case-law, therefore sets out a comprehensive set of principles and a framework for the assessment of mental capacity, along with a mechanism for decision-making on behalf of those individuals deemed to lack the capacity to do this for themselves. A further specific issue dealt with in the MCA, though overlooked in the majority of relevant socio-legal discourse, is the involvement in research of people lacking the capacity to consent to participation in research.

The Mental Capacity Act: implications for research

The MCA and related code of practice contain specific provisions concerning the participation in research of those adults lacking the capacity to consider their prospective participation, and to provide informed consent to such participation. Specifically, sections 30-34 of the act set out the duties for researchers, and the conditions under which people deemed to lack the capacity to consent may participate in research. This includes specifying the requirements for gaining ethical approval for such research (MCA, s30) and outlining a duty for researchers to consult with family members and/or others concerned with the welfare of the individual in question, as to whether the individual should participate in the proposed research (MCA, s32(4)(a)), and what the individual's wishes and feelings would be likely to be regarding participating in the proposed research, if they had the capacity in relation to this matter (MCA, s32(4)(b)).

The MCA code of practice provides further context for these issues, and also indicates a commitment to the involvement in research of people lacking the capacity to consent:

> 'It is important that research, involving people who lack capacity can be carried out, and that it is carried out properly. Without it, we would not improve our knowledge of what causes a person to lack or lose capacity, and the diagnosis, treatment, care and needs of people who lack capacity.'

(Department of Constitutional Affairs, 2007, p202)

The code may also be described as protective in nature, claiming that research involving people lacking capacity may only be carried out if there are reasonable grounds for believing that the research would not be so effective if only people with capacity were involved (Department of Constitutional Affairs, 2007, p206), and that the risk to any participants lacking capacity must be 'minimal', including concerning the risk of distress (Department of Constitutional Affairs, 2007, p209). It also states that research involving people lacking capacity must meet

---

2 [2016] EWCOP 53

one of the following two requirements: some chance of benefiting the person lacking capacity, and/or the aim of the research must be to provide knowledge about the cause of, or treatment or care of, people with the same impairing condition, or a similar condition (Department of Constitutional Affairs, 2007, p207). Importantly, this establishes the requirement for a nexus to exist between the impairment causing the lack of capacity to provide consent, and the focus of the proposed research.

Discussion

The priorities and competing agendas of autism research are core elements of the political discourses and tensions within the autistic and autism communities that have been described as the 'autism war'. Central to the contention between these opposing discourses is the issue of heterogeneity of intellectual and verbal ability apparent among the autistic population, and the resulting concerns to do with participation and representation, particularly around ensuring appropriate and sufficient representation of autistic people with co-morbid intellectual disability in autism-related research. I suggest that the legal framework of the MCA should be a key focus of emerging and developing political dialogue and debate within the autistic and autism communities around research priorities and agendas, and that this legal framework provides both challenges and opportunities.

Firstly, in terms of challenges posed by the MCA, it is possible that the language of the legislation – particularly that within the code of practice, which references 'diagnosis', 'cause', 'treatment' and 'cure' – may be perceived as problematic to those within the autistic and autism communities who understand autism to be a social and cultural identity to be enabled within society, rather than a 'disorder' in need of cure. Further, I consider that there is a significant need to explore empirically and to debate politically the role of family members and other individuals who act as consultees for autistic people who lack the ability to consent to research participation (as provided for in the MCA). There is scope for consultees to influence research participation, and therefore potentially the direction of autism research, which, given the range of differing opinions apparent around research priorities among different stakeholders within the autistic and autism communities, is an issue that warrants further consideration and debate.

Considering the opportunities presented by the MCA for informing and shaping discourse around autism-related research, I suggest particularly that the general principles underpinning the act – especially concerning the presumption of capacity, and the need to support capacious decision-making through all practicable steps provides a strong legal basis for the development of the emerging participatory agenda within autism research. Furthermore, where autistic individuals are deemed to lack the capacity to consent to participation, the protective agenda of the MCA provides a legal framework for the right to participation and representation, balanced with the minimisation of associated risk.

Discourses surrounding the politics of autism research are both topical and contentious. They are also inextricably linked with questions and concerns associated with participation and representation, capacity and informed consent. It is therefore of crucial importance that the legal framework of the MCA forms a key part of such emerging discourses, and that the challenges and opportunities it represents are explored and exploited to the greatest possible extent.

References

Barnes C (1996) Disability and the myth of the independent researcher. *Disability and Society* **11** (1) 107–110.

Charman T and Clare P (2004) *Mapping Autism Research: Identifying UK priorities for the future.* London: National Autistic Society.

Dawson G (2013) Dramatic increase in autism prevalence parallels explosion of research into its biology and causes. *Archives of General Psychiatry* **70** 9–10.

Department of Constitutional Affairs (2007) *The Mental Capacity Act 2005: Code of practice.* London: The Stationery Office.

Hodge N (2017) *Education System Should Help Autistic Pupils Achieve Potential* [online]. Sheffield: Sheffield Telegraph. Available at: http://www.sheffieldtelegraph.co.uk/news/opinion/education-education-system-should-help-autistic-pupils-achieve-potential-1-8365121 (accessed September 2017).

Krahn TT and Fenton A (2012) Funding Priorities: autism and the need for a more balanced research agenda in Canada. *Public Health Ethics* **5** 296–310.

Nind M and Searle J (2009) Concepts of access for people with learning disability: towards a shared understanding. *Disability and Society* **24** (3) 273–287.

Office for Autism Research Coordination, National Institute of Mental Health, on behalf of the Interagency Autism Coordinating Committee (IACC) (2012) *2010 IACC Autism Spectrum Disorder Research Portfolio Analysis Report* [online]. Available at: http://iacc.hhs.gov/portfolio-analysis/2010/index.shtml (accessed September 2017).

Oliver M (1992) Changing the social relations of research production. *Disability, Handicap and Society* **7** (2) 101–114.

Oliver M (1993) Redefining disability: A challenge to research. In: J Swain, V Finkelstein, and S French et al. (Eds) *Disabling Barriers: Enabling Environments.* London: SAGE Publications.

Participatory Autism Research Collective (2017) Website home page. Available at: https://participatoryautismresearch.wordpress.com (accessed September 2017).

Pellicano E, Dinsmore A & Charman T (2014) What should autism research focus upon? Community views and priorities from the United Kingdom. *Autism* **18** (7) 756–770.

Pitney J (2015) *The Politics of Autism: Navigating the contested spectrum.* Maryland: Rowman and Littlefield.

Shaping Autism Research in the UK (2017) *Aims of Series* [online]. Available at: http://www.shapingautismresearch.co.uk/post/111548874040/aims-of-series (accessed September 2017).

Singh J, Iles J & Lazzeroni L (2009) Trends in US autism research funding. *Journal of Autism and Developmental Disorders* **39** 788–795

Social Care Institute for Excellence (2016) *Mental Capacity Act 2005 at a Glance* [online]. Available at: https://www.scie.org.uk/publications/ataglance/ataglance05.asp (accessed September 2017).

Yergeau M (2013) Clinically significant disturbance: on theorists who theorize theory of mind [online]. *Disability Studies Quarterly* **33** (4). Available at: http://dsq-sds.org/article/view/3876/3405#top (accessed September 2017).

Engaging 'seldom-heard' individuals in participatory autism research

Professor Elizabeth Pellicano

Abstract

Everybody should have a say in the decisions that affect their lives – in schools, at work, in local communities and also in research. Yet autistic people and their family members are rarely actively engaged in the research process and many people feel disenfranchised as a result. Developing ways to actively involve autistic people and their allies in the research process – that is, conducting *participatory autism research* – is one key way to turn this situation around. But where does this leave individuals with additional intellectual disabilities and/or limited spoken communication, who are all too often marginalised by formal decision-making processes? In this chapter, I describe two research projects that sought to identify ways of supporting the inclusion of such individuals in the research process – methods that are critically person-centred and relational in nature. The results demonstrate that genuine participation in the research process by individuals with additional intellectual disabilities and/or limited spoken communication is not straightforward, but attempts to understand their way of seeing and acting in the world as best one can, from their perspective, can transform research with these 'seldom-heard' individuals.

Introduction

Autism directly or indirectly affects millions of citizens in the UK and across the globe. Despite widespread public interest in autism, autistic people and their families living in the UK have rarely been actively engaged in the research process. They have largely not been given the opportunity to decide research priorities, shape how an issue is researched, or help draw out practical lessons from research. Many have reported feeling disenfranchised as a result (Pellicano *et al*, 2014b; Milton, 2014). One promising way to turn this around is to conduct participatory autism research; involving autistic people directly in the research process – including those with additional intellectual disabilities and varying speech, language and communication needs.

In this chapter, I describe projects that sought to do just this – one with young disabled people, with and without a diagnosis of autism, educated and living within residential special schools in England (Pellicano *et al*, 2014c), and one with autistic adults within a supported living environment (Gaudion *et al*, 2015a; 2015b). These projects are unique in that they (1) focus on individuals who are so often excluded from research by virtue of their limited spoken communication and/or intellectual ability – the very focus of this edited volume, and (2) represent attempts to involve them in the research process itself.

The chapter begins with the background and rationale for autistic involvement in research, followed by a detailed overview of the two participatory research projects in which I have had the privilege of being involved and which serve to illustrate the extent and nature of participation with this particular group of autistic individuals, and its impact on research. I conclude by suggesting that, although the nature of participatory autism research may well differ for research involving autistic individuals with additional intellectual disabilities and/or limited spoken communication, the value of doing so is, if anything, greater still.

Shifting the landscape of autism research in the UK

There has been a dramatic expansion of autism research in the past decade in the UK and abroad (Dawson, 2013). In the most comprehensive review of UK autism research ever undertaken, my colleagues and I found that almost £21 million was invested in autism research between 2007 and 2011 by UK government and non-government organisations, spread across 106 different projects (Pellicano *et al*, 2013). Such investment is much welcomed, especially if the research is potentially capable of both enhancing our understanding of autism and enriching the lives of those who are autistic. Further analysis of the landscape of research funding showed, however, that the majority of UK research focused heavily on 'basic science' – neural and cognitive systems, genetics and other risk factors – instead of research targeting the immediate circumstances in which autistic people find themselves, on services, treatments and interventions and education. Moreover, respondents (n=1521) to a large-scale survey were dissatisfied with this distribution of current UK autism research. While autistic people and family members were impressed by the amount of work that goes into autism research and valued the investment in basic science, they were not convinced that research had made a real difference to their lives. Our participants wanted to see real changes for themselves, their child, or for the person with whom they work. In particular, they prioritised research that would (1) identify effective public services, (2) establish evidence-based interventions, and (3) understand the place of autistic people in society. They also called for more research on under-served populations, including autistic adults, and girls and women (Pellicano et al, 2014a; see also Wallace et al, 2013).

One reason for the mismatch between what was being researched and what people wanted to be researched was a lack of involvement in the decision-making processes that shape research and its applications. In other research fields, community involvement in research has been shown to be paramount to ensuring that research is (1) more thoroughly relevant to communities, (2) sufficiently tailored to the realities of their everyday lives, and (3) consistent with their values (Callard et al, 2012; Faridi et al, 2007). Yet autism researchers do not do this enough. According to our findings (Pellicano et al, 2014b), autistic people, their family members, and even practitioners, are rarely involved in the decision-making processes that shape research and its application (see also Pellicano et al, 2011; Wallace et al, 2013). Research priorities are therefore ordinarily set almost exclusively by funders and academics in specialist fields. This is problematic not least because of the feeling of exclusion that it engenders. Indeed, the same respondents to the large-scale survey described above provided largely negative descriptions of their interactions with researchers. Family members felt disappointed and frustrated at being 'mined' for information and having little or no opportunity to learn about the resulting discoveries and what they might mean for them, while autistic adults reported feeling objectified ('we are a bit like monkeys in a zoo') and their experiential expertise disregarded by researchers (Pellicano et al, 2014b). This lack of reciprocity resulted in feelings of distrust and disenfranchisement. Indeed, as one autistic adult said to me during the project; 'Whatever I say, is it really going to influence anyone?'.

Developing ways to involve autistic people and their allies – in deciding how an issue is researched, how it becomes funded, who undertakes the research and so on – is one key way both to rebuild feelings of trust and to ensure that a greater portion of research has a direct and sustained impact on those who need it most. In an attempt to shift the landscape of UK autism research towards more participatory research, a group of autistic and non-autistic researchers launched the Shaping Autism Research seminar series (www.shapingautismresearch.co.uk) funded by the Economic and Social Research Council (see Fletcher-Watson et al, in prep. for details). This seminar series sought to bring together (autistic and non-autistic) researchers and funders, and autistic people, their family members, and those who support them to work out ways of promoting autistic involvement in research. To this end, we held six seminars across England, Scotland and Wales with over 200 delegates. The seminars were highly participatory and interactive in nature and, critically, were inclusive. Indeed, autistic people represented one third to half of attendees.

The discussions across the seminars were many and varied – and sometimes emotionally charged. Seminar delegates repeatedly highlighted that the lived experiences of autistic people – their experiential expertise (Collins & Evans, 2002; Milton, 2014; Pellicano et al, 2011) – is neither apparent nor valued in the context of autism research. Consequently, these conversations gave rise to three core principles of participatory autism research:

1. Trust – that researchers must be honest and committed in their interactions.

2. Mutual respect – that autistic people and their allies need to feel respected (and for their views to be valued) by researchers.

3. Listening and learning – that researchers, both autistic and non-autistic, need to listen to and learn from the community's expertise and experience.

Seminar delegates also highlighted several barriers to participatory autism research (see Fletcher-Watson et al, in prep.), the most relevant to this chapter being the relative absence of the 'voices' of autistic people who have additional intellectual disabilities and/or limited spoken communication. This is an underserved population in current autism research, largely due to the challenges to non-autistic researchers in assessing them in traditional psychometric and experimental investigations (Tager-Flusberg & Kasari, 2013; Tager-Flusberg et al, 2016) and in eliciting their views and experiences.

Developing ways to include all autistic people in the research process

All individuals – including those with additional intellectual disabilities and/or limited spoken communication – have the right to shape the decisions that influence their lives, including research. Yet, the absence of both a shared (spoken) language and knowledge of the most effective ways of accessing these individuals' views (Goldbart et al, 2014; Hill et al, 2016; Ware, 2004) means that they are often marginalised from this process. It also means that supporting adults (parents, clinicians, educators) are often given the role of speaking on their behalf and making decisions in their (perceived) best interests, which, while potentially well-meaning, can also be paternalistic. In the section that follows, I describe two research projects (Gaudion et al, 2015a; 2015b; Pellicano et al, 2014c) that sought to identify creative ways of supporting the inclusion of autistic individuals with additional intellectual disabilities and/or limited spoken language in the research process.

The first of these projects examined the views and experiences of children and young people with special educational needs (including those who were autistic) living in residential special schools in England (Pellicano et al, 2014c; see also Greathead et al, 2016, and Hill et al, 2016). One key aim of the study was to determine whether their rights were being protected and promoted in these schools, including with regard to having a say in the decisions that affect their lives. Yet, accessing their views and experiences was not a straightforward process. The children residing in such schools are often the most vulnerable and marginalised children – those who are most severely disabled, who have the most complex needs and the greatest dependency on others. We therefore adopted participatory research techniques to ensure that we gained a fuller sense of their experiences – from their perspectives, not just the people supporting them.

We sought to place these children at the heart of the research process by setting up a Young Researchers' Group. This group helped to ensure that at least some of the young people could contribute to the design of the study, advise on data collection techniques, and help to steer the research process – and, critically, that their 'voices' were not subsumed by those of adults. The group included children and young people aged from 13 to 19 years old and reflected a wide range of special educational needs and disabilities, including: autism, severe learning difficulties, ADHD, social emotional and mental health needs, hearing impairment and the deaf, and those with limited spoken communication. During a series of workshops, they helped to identify key issues for investigation, advise on and pilot appropriate methodologies, verified the themes identified from the data, disseminate the findings (to government ministers at the House of Lords in December 2014) and make a short film of their experiences.

The diversity of the group meant that we needed to employ multiple methods to access their views and ensure that they influenced the research process, including allowing the children to communicate in the ways that best suited them – via drawing, writing, pictures and symbols (see Hill *et al*, 2016, for more detail). Indeed, the three workshops held across the 3-month project provided opportunities for the young people to comment and critique our then-proposed methods, including the questions for the interviews and focus groups and the nature of the various activities. On the basis of the young people's expert comments, we subsequently adjusted our methods to ensure that they reflected the needs and experiences of children and young people in residential special schools. Specifically, we (1) simplified and reduced the number of questions for the focus groups, (2) used widget symbols and images to make the interview questions more accessible, (3) tried to keep the size of focus groups small enough to ensure everyone had a chance to have a voice, (4) began focus group discussions with a written post-it activity to help generate ideas and to make sure that everyone had their say, even those who found it hard to speak for a variety of reasons and (5) dramatically simplified the consent form so that the young person's signature was the only written requirement and that they were supported to process the information contained in the information letter. The Young Researchers' Group were also asked to help summarise the main findings for a report that would be suitable for other young people, and an illustrator joined the group to help capture the process in comic-book form. In these ways, the Young Researchers had a significant impact on the nature of the research.

Yet the methods employed for our Young Researchers' Group and, subsequently, for many of the participants in our study, were not successful in accessing the experiences of those with particularly complex needs, including children and young people with severe-to-profound intellectual disabilities and/or limited spoken communication. For these children and young people, we instead used a combination of ethnographic and structured observation methods in order to build a picture of the ways in which they were able to express themselves and the extent and nature of adult support they received across a given day in their school. One researcher spent time with the child or young person from the beginning of the school day and/or at the 'home' part of school to gain information about their experiences, closely observing the young person's activities, interests and relationships with others – ultimately, to understand their perception of the world as best one can from their perspective. These methods allowed a fine-grained analysis of children's spontaneous communicative behaviour in naturalistic school and 'home' settings and of the way that these behaviours were recognized, interpreted, and responded to (or not) by their teachers and carers.

The short duration of this project (three months) meant that we could only gain a 'snapshot' of their lives in school. Nevertheless, we found that that children and young people with severe-to-profound intellectual disabilities and limited spoken communication have ways to make their intentions known, even though they may use idiosyncratic ways of doing so, through vocalisations, gestures and symbols, and that adults play important roles in supporting these children's bids for interaction (see Greathead *et al*, 2016, for more detail). These findings challenge prevailing assumptions that such young people 'have little agency, ability to voice experiences, or opportunity to participate in society' (Simmonds & Watson, 2014, p19), and suggest instead that they are active social agents when they receive the right support (Nind *et al*, 2010).

The second project (Gaudion *et al*, 2015a; 2015b) used similar ethnographic methods to involve autistic adults with additional intellectual disabilities and/or limited spoken communication in the design process. The length of this project (six years) meant that the person-centred methods employed went much deeper than in Pellicano *et al* (2014c). Gaudion's PhD work investigated autistic adults' unique relationships with their (supported living) environment with the aim of developing collaborative design tools for the adults themselves, their support staff and their family members (see Gaudion *et al*, 2015a; 2015b, for more detail). To do so, she adopted both person-centred and participatory methods, involving the views and experiences of multiple informants – the autistic adult, the designer, support staff, and family members to guide the design process.

Gaudion's starting point was that the physicality of the world and what it affords is critical for an autistic person's understanding of themselves, other people and the world around them – and, importantly, for others' understanding of them. She described how, during the design process, she visited the adults in their homes on multiples occasions, intensely observing the ways that they engaged with their environment, including in the garden, in the interior of their home and with everyday objects (e.g. washing machines, vacuum cleaners). Once she had gained the adults' trust, these initial observations were followed by interactions with the adults, where she mirrored their favourite activities, as a way of creating a reciprocal interaction (Nind & Hewett, 1994; see also Gernsbacher, 2006, for discussion), as described in the following diary entry:

> 'In time, the designer could see that Tom looked content and relaxed sitting quietly picking at the leather on his sofa ... Unable to ask Tom directly, "What do you like about doing that?" the designer then mirrored Tom's actions and experienced it for herself, which enabled her to externalise her thoughts and begin to understand and empathise with Tom: picking the leather off the sofa was surprisingly satisfying and could be equated to the satisfaction one gets from popping bubble wrap. So instead of a ruined sofa, the researcher now perceived Tom's sofa as an object wrapped in fabric that is fun to pick.'

(Gaudion *et al*, 2015a, p65).

Reflecting on these observations, Gaudion describes how her initial perception of Tom's home environment and the sofa in particular was one of 'destruction'. But it was only through her sustained interactions with Tom, where she got to know him, his (sensory) preferences and his unique affordances with the environment, which signalled his way of being in the world, that she began to see things anew, from his perspective. She explains that working with the adults in this way caused a shift in her thinking around design and human experience:

> 'What I consistently observed was their unique emotional response and interaction with the physical environment that was very different to my own. Experiences not prescribed around the social construct of the intended functionality of things, but instead representing different ways of being in the world that continuously challenged my own perceptual experience.'

(Gaudion, 2015a, p21).

That is, she began to explore the 'subjective significance of [autistic spectrum] related experiences' (Milton & Bracher, 2013, p64). She used these experiences, in addition to information obtained through conversations with support workers and family members, to design 'sensory preference cards' (a card-sorting task to help support workers understand the adults' sensory likes and dislikes), a 'tree of opportunity' (a visual map of the adults' interests), and personalised 'everyday objects' (including a bubble-blowing vacuum cleaner).

Gaudion's work is unique in at least two key ways. Firstly, she sought to create design tools for a group of individuals who are very much underserved in the field of autism research and even in the field of design (see, for example, Keay-Bright, 2007; Frauenberger et al, 2012, for excellent exceptions). Secondly, and more critically, her work adopted a strengths-based (rather than a deficit-based) approach, exploring a person's triad of strengths – their sensory preferences, special interests, and different action capabilities – to select and develop participatory design methods. Her foundation, then, was fundamentally in contrast to the vast majority of autism research, which is firmly rooted within a medical (deficit-based) model. Instead, she pursued her research as an 'empathetic scholar' (Osteen, 2008, p297; see also Kouprie & Sleeswijk Visser, 2009), concerned with conducting research that both respects the principles of ethical conduct and respects autistic difference and personhood (see also Frauenberger et al, 2012). In so doing, Gaudion broadened her perspective and 'interactional expertise' with autistic adults (see Milton, 2014) to an understanding of the sensory and perceptual experiences of the adults with whom she worked, overcoming what Milton (2012; 2014) calls 'the double empathy problem'.

Conclusion

In both of the research projects briefly described herein, the researchers made extensive efforts to access the views and experiences of autistic people with additional intellectual disabilities and/or limited spoken communication to inform the research process. The researchers engaged with autistic people by stepping beyond the traditional boundaries of participatory research methods, which are often dependent on written and spoken feedback, such as questionnaires, interviews and co-design workshops, and include individuals with stronger communication abilities than those who have complex communication needs (Nind, 2008; Walmsley & Johnson, 2003). Instead, the researchers sought to design activities and approaches that met the specific needs of the groups with whom they were working – connecting, communicating (in non-traditional ways), and building trust and empathy with each person – that is, putting in place the very principles of participatory autism research identified in the *Shaping Autism Research* seminar series.

The deviation from traditional participatory methods necessarily raises questions, for both studies, about the extent of the participants' degree of *participation* in the research process. For many models of participatory research (e.g. Arnstein, 1969; Hart, 1992; Israel et al, 2005; Shier, 2001; see also www.involve.org), community members are considered active agents, where the very process of their involvement has a positive impact upon the research (by producing more 'authentic' knowledge; Grover, 2004) and also empowers community members themselves. Yet, although some of the activities described for the autistic children (Pellicano et al, 2014c) and adults (Gaudion et al, 2015a; 2015b) could be regarded as meaningfully shared, their participation in the research process was for the most part rather passive in nature. Their involvement was also not without the involvement of significant others (teachers and carers; Pellicano et al, 2014c; support workers and family members: Gaudion et al, 2015a; 2015b). If these individuals were unable to understand the nature of their involvement, can the work be described as genuinely participatory? While there are no straightforward answers to this question, it is clear from the brief descriptions provided that their participation in these projects was far from tokenistic. In both projects, the participants' interactions with the people supporting them (Pellicano et al, 2014) and with their environment (Gaudion et al, 2015a; 2015b) critically revealed their way of seeing and acting in the world – and their experiences ultimately shaped the researchers' perspectives, the research outputs and conclusions.

For many autistic children, young people and adults with additional intellectual disabilities and/or limited spoken communication, the nature of their differences will preclude their active involvement in participatory autism research. But this should not render them invisible to autism researchers. As the results from the projects described herein clearly attest, these individuals' experiences have so much to offer to the research process – beyond what can be said on their behalf. Researchers need to listen and learn from these individuals by develop trusting and authentic relationships with them in order to gain insight into their ways of being, which otherwise 'may not be immediately apparent to non-[autism spectrum] observers' (Milton & Bracher, 2013, p64). Only then will we get the much-needed research that is more relevant to the lives of these 'seldom-heard' individuals and tailored to their specific needs.

Acknowledgements

I am very grateful to all of the children, young people and adults, their families and their teaching or support staff, who so very generously gave up their time to be involved in these studies; to Damian Milton, for helpful comments on a previous version of this chapter; and to the following friends and colleagues for their continued constructive – and inspiring – conversations and overall dedication to participatory autism research: Jon Adams, Peter Beresford, Mel Bovis, Kabie Brook, Tony Charman, Ben Connors, Laura Crane, Abigail Croydon, James Cusack, Katie Gaudion, Scot Greathead, Vivian Hill, Lorcan Kenny, Sue Leekam, Joseph Long, Richard Mills, Damian Milton, Ari Ne'eman, Jeremy Parr, Susie Ridout, Marc Stears, Robyn Steward, Rhiannon Yates and Sue Fletcher-Watson. This work was supported by a Philip Leverhulme Prize from the Leverhulme Trust and a research seminar series grant from the Economic and Social Research Council (ES/M00225X/1).

References

Arnstein S (1969) A ladder of citizen participation. *Journal of the American Institute of Planners* **35** 216–224.

Callard F, Rose D & Wykes T (2012) Close to the bench as well as at the bedside: involving service users in all phases of translational research. *Health Expectations* **15** 389–400.

Collins HM & Evans R (2002) The third wave of science studies: studies of expertise and experience. *Social Studies of Science* **32** 235–296.

Dawson G (2013) Dramatic increase in autism prevalence parallels explosion of research into its biology and causes. *Archives of General Psychiatry* **70** 9–10.

Faridi Z, Grunbaum JA, Sajor Gray B, Franks A & Simoes E (2007) Community-based participatory research: next steps. *Preventing Chronic Disease* **4** 1–5.

Fletcher-Watson S, Adams J, Leekam S, Milton D, Parr J, Charman T & Pellicano E (in prep.) Making the future together: shaping autism research through meaningful participation. Manuscript in preparation.

Frauenberger C, Good J & Alcorn A (2012) Challenges, opportunities and future perspectives in including children with disabilities in the design of interactive technology. In: IDC '12: *Proceedings of the 11th International Conference on Interaction Design and Children*, 12-15 June 2012, Bremen, Germany pp 367-370. New York: ACM Press.

Gaudion K (2015) *A Designer's Approach: Exploring how autistic adults with additional learning disabilities experience their home environment*. PhD thesis. London, UK: Royal College of Art.

Gaudion K, Hall A, Myerson J & Pellicano L (2015a) Design and wellbeing: bridging the empathy gap between neurotypical designers and autistic adults. In: M Mani and P Kandachar (Eds) *Design for Sustainable Well-being and Empowerment* (pp 61–77). IISc Press and TU Delft.

Gaudion K, Hall A, Myerson J & Pellicano E (2015b) A designer's approach: how can autistic adults with learning disabilities be involved in the design process? *CoDesign: International Journal of CoCreation in Design and the Arts* **11** 49–69.

Gernsbacher MA (2006) Toward a behavior of reciprocity. *Journal of Developmental Processes* **1** 139–152.

Goldbart J, Chadwick D & Buell S (2014) Speech and language therapists' approaches to communication intervention with children and adults with profound and multiple learning disability. *International Journal of Language and Communication* **49** 687–701.

Greathead S, Yates R, Hill V, Kenny L, Croydon A & Pellicano E (2016) Supporting children with severe-to-profound learning difficulties and complex communication needs to make their views known: observation tools and methods. *Topics in Language Disorders* **36** 217–244.

Grover S (2004) '"Why won't they listen to us?" On giving power and voice to children participating in social research'. *Childhood* **11** 81–93.

Hart RA (1992) *Children's Participation: From tokenism to citizenship*. Florence: UNICEF.

Hill V, Croydon A, Greathead S, Kenny L, Yates R & Pellicano E (2016) Research methods for educational psychologists: developing techniques to facilitate all children and young people to have a 'voice'. *Educational and Child Psychology* **33** 26–43.

Israel BA, Parker EA, Rowe Z, Salvatore A, Minkler M, López J, Butz A, Mosley A, Coates L, Lambert G, Potito PA, Brenner B, Rivera M, Romero H, Thompson B, Coronado G & Halstead S (2005) Community-based participatory research: lessons learned from the centers for children's environmental health and disease prevention research. *Environmental Health Perspectives* **113** 1463–1471.

Keay-Bright W (2007) The reactive colours project: demonstrating participatory and collaborative design methods for the creation of software for autistic children. *Design Principles and Practices: An International Journal* **1** 28–35.

Kouprie M & Sleeswijk Visser F (2009) A framework for empathy in design: stepping into and out of the user's life. *Journal of Engineering Design* **20** 437–448.

Milton DEM (2012) On the ontological status of autism: the 'double empathy problem'. *Disability and Society* **27** 883–887.

Milton DEM (2014) Autistic expertise: a critical reflection on the production of knowledge in autism studies. *Autism* **18** 794–802.

Milton DEM & Bracher M (2013) Autistics speak but are they heard? *Medical Sociology Online* **7** 61–69.

Milton D, Mills R & Pellicano E (2014) Ethics and autism: where is the autistic voice? Commentary on Post et al. *Journal of Autism and Developmental Disorders* **44** 2650–2651.

Nind M (2008) *Conducting Qualitative Research with People with Learning, Communication and Other Disabilities: Methodological challenges* [online]. ESRC National Centre for Research Methods. Available at: http://eprints.ncrm.ac.uk/491/ (accessed September 2017).

Nind M, Flewitt R & Payler J (2010) The social experience of early childhood for children with learning disabilities: inclusion competence and agency. *British Journal of Sociology of Education* **31** 653–670.

Nind M & Hewett D (1994) *Access to Communication: Developing the basics of communication with people with severe learning difficulties through Intensive Interaction*. London: David Fulton.

Osteen M (2008) *Autism and Representation*. New York: Routledge.

Pellicano E, Dinsmore A & Charman T (2013) *A Future Made Together: Shaping autism research in the UK*. London: Institute of Education.

Pellicano E, Dinsmore A & Charman T (2014a) What should autism research focus upon? Community views and priorities from the UK. *Autism* **18** 756–770.

Pellicano E, Dinsmore A & Charman T (2014b) Views on researcher-community engagement in autism research in the United Kingdom: a mixed-methods study. *PLOS One*. DOI: 10.1371/journal.pone.0109946.

Pellicano E, Hill V, Croydon A, Greathead S, Kenny L & Yates R with Wac Arts (2014c) *My Life at School: Understanding the experiences of children and young people with special educational needs in residential special schools*. London, UK: Office of the Children's Commissioner. Available at: http://crae.ioe.ac.uk/post/104844796448/my-life-at-school

(accessed September 2017).

Pellicano E, Ne'eman A & Stears M (2011) Engaging, not excluding: a reply to Walsh et al. *Nature Reviews Neuroscience* **12** 769.

Pellicano E & Stears M (2011) Bridging autism, science and society: moving towards an ethically-informed approach to autism research. *Autism Research* **4** 271–282.

Shier H (2001) Pathways to participation: opening, opportunities and obligations. *Children and Society* **15** 107–117.

Tager-Flusberg H & Kasari C (2013) Minimally verbal school-aged children with autism spectrum disorder: the neglected end of the spectrum. *Autism Research* **6** 468-478.

Tager-Flusberg H, Plesa-Skwerer D, Joseph RM, Brukilacchio B, Decker J, Eggleston B, Meyer S & Yoder A (2016) Conducting research with minimally verbal participants with autism spectrum disorder. *Autism*, doi: 10.1177/1362361316654605.

Wallace S, Parr J & Hardy A (2013) *One in a Hundred: Putting families at the heart of autism research*. London, UK: Autistica.

Walmsley J & Johnson K (2003) *Inclusive Research with People with Learning Disabilities: Past, present, and futures*. London: Jessica Kingsley Publishers.

Ware J (2004) Ascertaining the views of people with profound and multiple learning disabilities. *British Journal of Learning Disabilities* **32** 175–179.

Refocusing: what you see isn't all there is – getting healthcare right in hospitals for autistic and learning disabled people

Jim Blair
Mary Busk, *expert by parental experience*
Simon Hawtrey-Woore, *expert by parental experience*
Ismail Kaji, *expert by lived and parental experience*
Ciara Lawrence, *expert by lived experience*
Gail Moody, *expert by parental experience*
Yvonne Newbold, *expert by parental experience*
Lauretta Ofulue, *expert by parental experience*

Being autistic and learning disabled means travelling through the maze of life that is geared towards people who are neither, and this can be very difficult. The multi-sensory stimulations, lights, noise and apparent endless questions, as well as misinterpretations of what is being communicated and what is being received, frequently make the world a challenging place with which to engage. Traversing healthcare systems and structures is hard for many of us. It can be like reading instructions in a language you do not understand and being expected to follow the set route, whether or not it suits you, in order to attend the appointment that is booked in your name.

The voice of experience

This chapter will focus on seeking to reset the lens for health professionals and others to enable them to gain insight into how to ensure each encounter is a positive one leading to better experiences and care outcomes. The voice of experts by lived and parental experience are throughout the chapter acting as guides in how to get care right. When the recipient of healthcare is using forms of communication other than speech, the practitioner will need to pay close, patient and careful attention and take their lead from the individual and the people who know them best.

Ciara has a learning disability and works at Mencap, here she talks about what is important to her when interacting with health services.

> 'Having accessible information understanding what is being said to me. I get anxious….I need reassurance of what is going to happen. It is hard in dentists and hospitals. I have a learning disability they need to be clear with me need to be consistent. I asked for reasonable adjustments and then I got them…being able to say how I felt. This was when I had a wisdom tooth taken out. I saw the chair and had a meltdown. The dentist said do you want to have it today or come in another time and we will put you to sleep. That was a positive experience. A small thing to make a big impact like having my mother with me when I had a GA [general anaesthetic].'

Ciara talked about how small things can make all the difference. Ismail has had some similar experiences to Ciara, both as a man who has a learning disability and as a father of young children.

> 'Health staff need to change attitudes, way they speak not jargon medical terms speak slowly...think about how the person/parent is feeling...communicate with patients. Don't rush things. Remember people will be nervous. Explain things in order it is difficult to remember things. It is helpful to use visual examples like pictures, showing what could be used....and then checking understanding. I would like to call after to check what was said because I forget what was said.'

The complexities of navigating healthcare services and settings can be very traumatic for autistic individuals with learning disabilities and their parents. There are however occasions when things go very well, but experience would suggest that this is not always at the start of the journey.

Pain cannot always be seen but that does not mean it is not felt

Lauretta illustrates how her four-year-old learning disabled autistic son, Otito, appears to express pain in 'atypical' ways. Here she discusses experiences with Otito when he was in hospital with pancreatitis.

> 'The pain charts recorded higher scores for pain based on normal responses. For example screaming, being irritable and displaying active movements especially kicking to show pain was ranked highly. They could not justify the need to give the level of pain relief I was requesting since the pain scores they charted did not support my claim.

> However, given his status as a severely autistic child with learning disabilities it was really not far-fetched. As time went by my son became very withdrawn. While what the health professionals saw was more of a quiet boy, what I saw was less of my child and more of a chronic patient. To them his quietness was only a confirmation that he was after all unwell.

> The learning disability nurse was very helpful and approachable. I was able to discuss my concerns easily with him. It was relieving to find someone – a health professional who finally understood my son's plight. He simply got it! The pain responses that I described to him were anything but alien. In fact he said it was quite common with children who had the level of autism that Otito possessed. It was also a relief to know that my son was neither alone nor was his case beyond redemption. The new pain document accommodated my son's unique responses to pain. Things (like being quiet, curling up in a foetal position, not moving around, staying in corners, grinding his teeth, closing his eyes even while awake, interacting less with people or toys etc) that were previously being overlooked were not only taken into account but in fact given higher scores using the new pain score sheet. It helped the doctors understand my son better. By using this new pain score sheet they could also justify the need for a higher level of pain relief (something that was also an important requirement for dispensing them).'

Seeing the whole person – the hospital passport

Being able to understand a person is essential in order to know how to meet their needs. Lauretta suggests that hospital passports can play a central role in this process. The hospital passport shaped a better experience of hospital care for Otito and has been effective for others.

> 'The learning disability nurse also made us aware of something called a "hospital passport". By the time I had filled out a "hospital passport" for him, it served as a well-documented description of nearly everything pertaining to my son. It was also an introductory piece of document that saved a lot of time by acquainting Health Care Professionals with my son's unique characteristics before an actual interaction.

> I was able to record everything from important information (like my son's name, date of birth, hospital number, NHS number, his weight, his height) to seemingly less important information (like his mealtimes, his sleep times, bath times, walk times) and silly information (like his favourite toy – for example his tablet, and the need to make sure it always had power, the things that worked – for example giving him his toy stethoscope before carrying out observations, things you must never do – for example administer his medicines without showing him the tray). I was also able to include many of the less important but routine activities that could set him off if not followed to the letter.

> As a severely autistic child understanding and applying information about all these activities were sometimes the difference between a good and bad day for Otito. These were the things he understood. They also provided him with stability and kept him feeling safe. Having the "hospital passport" was a relief to me as a parent because not only could I have a copy, I could leave one in his hospital file.'

Our NHS learning disability autism success story – a dental experience

Yvonne describes here a successful encounter with the NHS with her son Toby, a young man who has autism and severe learning disabilities.

> 'Of all the squillions of NHS appointments that we've clocked up over the years, seeing his dentist has to be the least stressful and the most enjoyable.

> However, Toby doesn't really make it easy for them. His favourite moment is always if he's able to outwit them and take control of the chair moving buttons himself.

> Toby is profoundly disabled, and he has the cognitive functioning level of a neuro-typical two year old. He is nonverbal, he has autism and he also has extreme oral sensitivity issues. He was tube fed completely until he was a teenager, and so he finds it almost impossible

to tolerate anything in his mouth, nor does he have the comprehension to understand why co-operating with the dentist is a good idea.

They [the dental team] ask for our help and then welcome it to keep Toby relaxed and happy throughout the appointment singing his favourite songs, letting him watch Mr Tumble on his iPad. They just "get it". They understand that people with learning disabilities or autism or both can perceive everything just that little bit differently. They know that trying to reason with Toby, or getting stern and officious, will simply not work. Most of all, they grasp that …the whole time Toby is the most important person in the room.

Toby has a very traumatic medical history stretching right back to when he was born. Most of his first six years were spent in hospital, and it was never expected he'd ever survive more than a few more weeks. None of us dared hope that we'd ever have him long enough to celebrate his 22nd birthday, which we did earlier this year.

Although his health is no longer as volatile as it once was – cannulating Toby is never easy, and now that he's bigger and stronger and able to resist much more, we weren't even sure if they'd be able to manage to sedate him. Of course we also knew that we would be meeting a new team, people we didn't know and who didn't know Toby. Another concern was that Toby now lives in a care home which can make my role as his no-longer-full-time-carer an awkward one, particularly with a new team who don't know Toby.

The appointment went wonderfully well. Two of the three staff members had never met Toby before, but that didn't matter because they understood how essential it is to make him feel important. They asked me questions, they involved all of us in Toby's care, and they made him feel welcome, happy and valued. They listened to any of our suggestions and then they followed them. Everything was about Toby and making it work well for him. They even chose to start the sedation process with nasal Midazolam, to cut down any distress caused by vein hunting with needles.

Toby can't talk so he has no way of telling us if he had toothache. He could be in excruciating pain and although his behaviour might indicate that he was in some way unwell, it would take us days, weeks or even longer to ascertain that it was tooth related. Even once we had worked it out, he wouldn't co-operate with a full dental examination, and it would take a lot of further planning and preparation to admit him to hospital for dental work under anaesthetic. Now, for the first time in his life, I have the reassurance of knowing that every six months minor problems will almost certainly be picked up before they escalate into full-scale extremely painful toothache.'

'Why isn't there a designated and highly trained team of learning disability specialists available for blood tests or X-rays or A & E admissions? Why can't every NHS team understand the importance of including the family and carers in every care-based decision regarding people with learning disabilities? Why can't every NHS appointment for Toby be long enough to work at gaining his trust and getting the best possible level of co-operation from him?'

Four simple steps could make all the difference

Yvonne Newbold suggests four straightforward steps to improve access to healthcare (http://yvonnenewbold.com/our-nhs-learning-disability-success-story/). She also offered her services to educate health practitioners. Her four suggestions are:

'**1. Involve** the families and carers in all learning disability care.

2. Actively invite and listen to suggestions and ideas from families and carers, and then **follow their lead.**

3. Factor in extra time at every appointment.

4. Ensure all staff have the patience, kindness, understanding and training to work with anyone with a learning disability.'

The four steps to getting it right as outlined by Yvonne are simple, but as her story of Toby's experience shows, they can be highly effective.

Simon and Mary continue the theme in their reflections on what works well for Simon's daughter Scarlett and Mary's son Alex.

Understand what makes someone tick

Scarlett is 11 years old and has severe learning disabilities and multi-sensory processing difficulties. Having a hospital appointment can be frightening, but for patients with a learning disability and who are autistic, this is magnified due to their difficulty with interpreting, making sense of and accepting what's going on.

Simon explains:

'Scarlett has no attention span and has sensory sensitivity. She can't filter anything out, so when she goes onto a ward, she is overwhelmed by the people, machines, colours and noises.'

Tapping into the knowledge of parents and supporters is vital in order to tune into the individual and to see the whole picture.

Reflections on what works: understanding the whole picture

Mary:

'Alex, our severely learning disabled son with autism, is now 17. Our best experiences of healthcare have been when people have cared about us and about Alex. Learning disability nurses have been a highlight because we have not had to explain Alex to them. They have understood his communication, behaviour and health needs instinctively.

Alex's ear nose throat (ENT) surgery when he was younger was good because we were able to get the right medical care for his needs. Getting grommits and having his tonsils and adenoids removed greatly improved his overall health. Before that he was chronically sick and lived on antibiotics. We explained to medical professionals that as our son had such severe problems with language and communication for example, we wanted his physical health to be as good as possible. Otherwise coping with very poor health would make efforts to develop his language, communication and learning much harder. They understood this. That personal understanding and empathy from the ENT consultant in particular meant that we could call on him when other crises arose as he got older. That is because that consultant understood the whole picture for our son, that he could not speak or indicate pain or say what the matter was.

The possible becoming impossible then possible again

'As Alex got older we thought things would get easier but they became more difficult. The possible became impossible – such as blood tests and cooperating with many procedures. A poor experience of our son being asked to leave a hospital because he was considered a health and safety risk eventually became a positive experience. With the support of a learning disability nurse he had a number of procedures done at once and we arranged for sedation before and on admission to hospital.'

Always a person – it's a principle and a right

'We have sensed sometimes that because our son cannot speak that somehow he seems to be less of a person to some people. This leads to our need to advocate strongly for the best possible care for our son as we would expect for ourselves and everyone else. A second key principle is to have a preventative and early intervention approach so ensuring that health issues do not develop. A third key principle is that his needs should be met with the right services. For example Alex still needs therapy input from physiotherapy, occupational therapy and speech and language therapy to ensure that he is able to communicate, develop good physical health and manage his sensory needs as well as possible.'

The issues raised and reflected on by Mary are essential in order to provide care in health settings that effectively meet the needs of autistic people with a learning disability and their families.

Gail discusses some key issues in relation to how good care is not about fitting people into the system but making adaptations. Gail is the mother of a young teenage girl with multiple sensory and processing issues as well as numerous health challenges.

One size does not fit all – good experiences

Gail:

'A good experience for any child with a learning disability is one that is child centred, inclusive and as individualised as the setting allows. A situation in which the health workers understand and respect the fact that just because different children may have the same disability doesn't mean that a 'one size fits all' approach is either acceptable or workable.

Generally small adjustments in the way the clinics, wards etc. are run when combined with education about and an understanding of generally acceptable codes of practice will make the visits as positive and manageable as possible for all concerned.

An example of a positive and productive hospital visit is: the staff had read my daughter's personal passport and were aware of her complex needs and the best way in which to approach her. She is deaf/blind, has multi-sensory impairment and Down's syndrome amongst other things. The staff were aware of her sensory issues and were mindful of not overcrowding her and offered her a quiet space if that would make the whole experience both more accessible and more tolerable for her. The consultant actually asked how close he needed to get so that she could see him talking to her! He also took time to listen to her questions and answered her rather than talk directly to me. This made her feel totally included and a valued part of the whole process, that she could make a decision about what was happening to her rather than simply being the person to whom things were done.'

What would health professionals benefit from knowing and doing?

- Listen to the parents, they are the experts in their children.
- Know the distance at which they can safely interact with the child, young person or adult whilst still respecting their space.
- Understand that it is not appropriate to approach people from behind and surprise them with a hand on their shoulder.
- Be aware that many people with learning disabilities and autism find it almost impossible to filter out sensory stimulation.

Ismail and Ciara came up with the following points:

- Understand the person.
- Be patient and calm.
- Be supportive in the best way for that person.
- Adjust your thinking and focus.
- Know that small things make a big difference.
- Build in extra time.
- Give clear instructions.

→ Avoid jargon.

→ Break things down – what is going to happen, when, how and who will be involved?

T.E.A.C.H

In order to ensure care is adjusted to meet a person with learning disabilities' specific needs, a TEACH approach, first developed in Hertfordshire by the community learning disability team, is required:

Time – take time to work with the person.

Environment – alter the environment to meet the person's needs, for example, by providing quieter areas, reducing lighting and minimising waiting times.

Attitude – have a positive, solutions-orientated focus.

Communication – find out the best way to communicate with the person and their family, carers and supporters, and also communicate this to colleagues.

Help – consider what help the person and their family, carers and supporters need, and how can you meet these needs.

(Blair *et al*, 2016)

Conclusion

Small differences can lead to big changes which can escalate if carried out by many people on numerous occasions. Big changes in how autistic people with a learning disability access and experience healthcare can and should be informed by stakeholders, including the patient and their family.

Blair *et al* (2016) identified the following simple steps:

→ Take time to be with the person and their families to understand their lived experiences.

→ Pick up not only on what is said, but also what is not said, and avoid hurrying the interaction.

It is essential to remember the every interaction counts and each contact matters. Health professionals only spend a fraction of time with a person, so it is vital to gain as much insight as possible from the person and those who know them best, and to consider all that is being relayed, verbally and nonverbally. In doing so, healthcare practitioners can refocus how they interpret what they see and develop their understanding that what is seen superficially is not all that there is.

Reference

Blair J, Busk M, Goleniowska H, Hawtrey-Wore S, Morrus S, Mewbols Y & Nimmo S (2016) Through our eyes: what parents want for their children from health professionals. In: S Hardy, E Chaplin and P Woodward (Eds) *Supporting the Physical Health Needs of People with Learning Disabilities* (pp197–212). Brighton: Pavilion Publishing and Media Ltd.

Useful websites and resources

British Institute of Learning Disabilities (BILD)
www.bild.org.uk
The institute helps develop the organisations that provide services, and the people who give support.

Books Beyond Words
www.booksbeyondwords.co.uk
Publishes accessible stories in pictures to help people with learning and communication disabilities explore and understand their own experiences.

Disability Matters
www.disabilitymatters.org.uk
An e-learning resource to enhance understanding and skills of staff.

Down's Side Up
www.downsideup.com
Gently changing perceptions of Down's syndrome.

Easyhealth
www.easyhealth.org.uk
Provides over 250 free accessible leaflets, health guides and videos.

Mencap
http://www.bacdis.org.uk/policy/documents/Gettingitright.pdf
A group of organisations working towards better healthcare, well-being and quality of life for people with a learning disability.

NHS Choices, *Going into Hospital with a Learning Disability*
http://www.nhs.uk/Livewell/Childrenwithalearningdisability/Pages/Going-into-hospital-withlearning-disability.aspx
Information on preparing a person with a learning disability for hospital.

University of Hertfordshire
http://www.intellectualdisability.info/
Understanding learning disability and health.

Other useful reading

Blair J, Anthony T, Gunther I, Hambley Y, Harrison N, Lambert N & Stuart C (2017) A protocol for the preparation of patients for theatre and recovery. *Learning Disability Practice* **20** (2) 22–26.

Blair J (2017) What you see isn't all there is…understanding people with learning disabilities and health issues. *Care Talk* **62** June 17 12.

Blair J (2017) Diagnostic overshadowing: see beyond the diagnosis. *British Journal of Family Medicine* Jan/Feb **17** 34–35.

Towards meaningful participation in research and support practice: effecting change in autism services

Dr Joseph Long and Alastair Clarkson

Abstract

This chapter outlines ways in which practice research within an autism service provider has directed attention towards meaningful participation in decisions about support. The authors share insights from an action research project on voice and involvement as well as efforts to meaningfully engage supported people in an organisation-wide survey of service experience. In so doing we aim to demonstrate that inclusive support practice and inclusive research practice can usefully inform one another.

Introduction

There is an ethical imperative for professionals in both autism support services and autism research to involve autistic people more meaningfully in defining priorities and directing practice. This chapter describes the ways in which a research programme embedded within autism support services has been harnessed to direct an organisational focus on autistic involvement in service provision. Here we share ways in which inclusive survey methods and participatory action research can enable and respond to the voices of autistic people that have additional intellectual disabilities.

In documenting initiatives to better include autistic people with intellectual disabilities in decisions about their lives, we have also had an opportunity to develop research processes that are themselves more inclusive and participatory than is common in autism research. It is our contention that inclusive support practice and inclusive research practice can usefully inform one another.

The authors of this chapter are employed as resident researchers within Scottish Autism, a third-sector autism service provider. In this role we undertake research that is rooted in day-to-day support practice in order to inform practice development. We wish to be clear from the outset that the dominant authorial voices in this particular chapter are those of researchers with backgrounds in support practice, and that this position informs our perspective. Our aim here is to share ways in which professional practices focused on enabling and facilitating individual voices are changing the wider culture of our organisation and how we, as researchers, are moving toward greater collaboration and co-production.

The participation agenda in support practice and research

In recent decades policy debates and legislation in the UK have featured moves to increase citizen and 'user' participation in the running of public services, including health and social care provision (e.g. Department of Health, 2001, 2002, 2007; HM Government, 2007; The Scottish Government, 2013). The broad disability rights movement has long advocated a shift from paternalistic models of care to services that are shaped by the aspirations of supported people and actively involve individuals in discussions and decisions about their lives (see Barnes & Mercer, 2006; Beresford & Campbell, 1994; Oliver, 1990). Self-advocates and professionals working in the fields of autism and intellectual disability have further impressed the need to redress the power relationships inherent in professional support contexts towards greater equality and self-determination for supported people (e.g. Duffy, 2003; Murray, 2016). As Duffy (2003:p5) states, 'Put simply, if you have self-determination then this means you are in charge of your own life. If you do not have self-determination then other people are in charge of you'.

The field of autism research has been slower to involve autistic people in priority-setting and taking a meaningful role in research processes. The 2013 report *A Future Made Together* (Pellicano *et al*, 2013) highlighted the fact that autistic people and their families wished to see a greater research focus on the services that they receive, and that research participants often had little input into research questions. Moreover, those that participated in research often did not get to see the results or outcomes from the research in which they had participated. Calls for greater participation in research are gaining traction, particularly from the autistic community (e.g. Chown *et al*, 2017; Milton & Bracher, 2013).

Having a resident research capacity within an organisation provides the opportunity to create a programme of research rooted in the day-to-day concerns and priorities of the autistic people that we support, and to involve autistic people meaningfully in research processes. In this respect practitioners and supported people are not just users of research, seeking to translate and apply academic research findings into support practice, rather we look to generate research evidence from day-to-day support practice and the lived experience of autistic people in order to better understand how services can ensure the well-being of the people that they support.

Although many autistic individuals are vocal and articulate self-advocates, individuals with additional intellectual disabilities often require significant personalised support, augmentative communication, and patient, well-planned engagement to enable their voices to be heard. Without the input of these specialist supports, communication differences associated with autism, often encountered alongside significant intellectual disability, can result in individuals facing exclusion from processes of consultation and research.

Underpinning our approach has been an organisation-wide discussion about the importance of recognising and listening to supported peoples' voices. This invokes a need to understand and enable an individual's unique mode of communication and the recognition that voice may take many forms. It also connotes a second meaning of voice – that of having a say and being heard in decisions about support practice and service management (Long *et al*, 2017).

Meaningful survey participation: listening and responding to autistic voice

A recent initiative at Scottish Autism has been an organisation-wide survey of supported people in order to understand the experience of services and to identify areas for improvement. Whilst this kind of assessment should take place constantly within individual services through everyday discussions and formal review processes, a larger-scale survey allows an organisation to establish systemic strengths and areas for improvement identified by supported people. The survey team comprised the organisation's researchers, practitioners and a panel of supported autistic people who advised and piloted the survey materials.

Whilst a questionnaire was circulated to those supported people that were able to answer in writing, we also developed an individualised interview process to better enable the participation of adults with different communication styles. The team did not feel that standardised, written questionnaires would provide a vehicle for effective engagement of many autistic people with intellectual disabilities supported in Scottish Autism's services. We also felt that existing survey examples we obtained appeared inadequate for the task: we did not consider that putting smiley faces or symbols next to a standard written question constituted being 'autism friendly'. Rather, we sought to create adapted and individualised interview processes in order to suit the communication style of each participant.

The team devised the survey process according to the principle that meaningful engagement of a representative sample of supported individuals was thought to be preferable to a tokenistic engagement of all the people that we support. Accordingly, we undertook the survey with a sample of just over 10 percent of supported people within our services (43 people using both forms of the survey) and sought an in-depth engagement. Participants in the adapted interview were selected at random and we aimed to engage every selected person in some way. Even if participants ultimately found it difficult or impossible to participate, we offered the opportunity based around successive attempts at adaptation. Understanding our own limited view of the minds of others, we did not accept any perception of an individual's capacity to communicate as a reason not to attempt engagement. Rather, we felt the onus to be on the team to find an appropriate method of engagement, even if only a small number of questions could be completed.

Personalised support for people with autism and intellectual disabilities requires an understanding of individuals' unique thinking style and communication profile. Enabling support relationships also respond to a person's personality, interests and motivations. A meaningful research engagement must do likewise if it is to understand how well a person is being supported to achieve a good quality of life. Interviewers therefore worked closely with service teams and supported individuals to assess communication profiles, interests and motivations, to get to know the participants, and ensure that supported people felt comfortable with the process. As Dinah Murray (2016) has argued, sharing individual interests and motivation with supported people is an important means of building trust and establishing positive relationships. Interviewers spent time talking about individual interests with participants and incorporating these into survey design. For example one rating scale featured images from the film *Aladdin* to denote positive or negative responses, another young man who enjoys quizzes followed a quiz format with the interviewer with rounds and prizes (though it was made clear there were no 'right' answers). One part of the survey then asked about how far support teams invested in these individual interests with the individual. Familiarisation, aimed at building rapport and establishing a positive relationship to support the survey process, often took place over several sessions and the survey was occasionally broken up into separate sessions to avoid fatigue or overwhelming individuals. The average time spent on each interview, including familiarisation, was 7.5 hours.

Rather than ask identically-worded questions of all participants, the team sought to rate services against a set of common indicators. These indicators referred to the organisation's own framework for ethical practice and the Association for Real Change's *Charter for Involvement* (Association for Real Change, 2015) – a set of practice guidelines for participation and involvement created by people with intellectual disabilities in Scotland. We asked supported people about seven elements of their support, each aligning with Scottish Autism's framework for ethical practice:

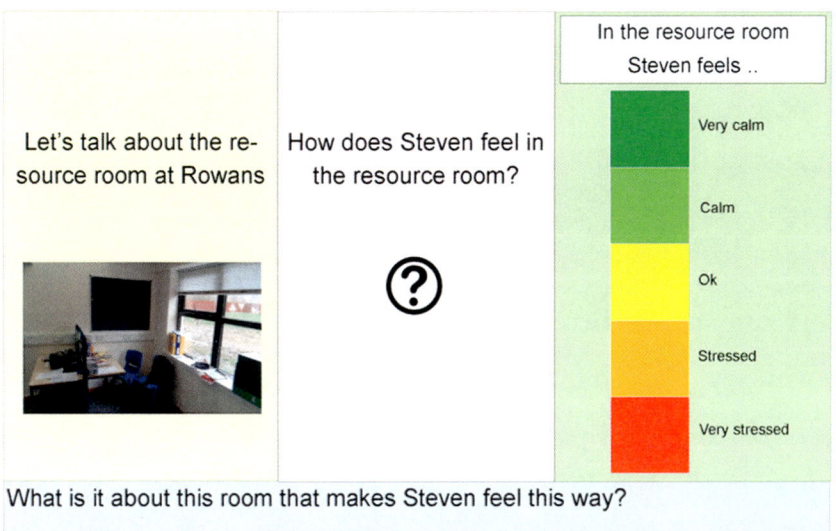

Figure 1. Example of the adapted interview survey format

→ Support for health and well-being.
→ Positive relationships and social opportunities.
→ Support for communication and involvement.
→ Understanding of diverse thinking styles.
→ Low stress service environments.
→ Shared understandings of support and goals.
→ Continuous learning for everybody.

For example, in asking about 'communication and involvement' we looked for indicators of whether individuals or their support practitioners decide on daily activities; whether individuals play a role in recruitment to their services; what input individuals have into their support plan; and whether supported people felt able to make a complaint about their service.

Questions established concrete, rather than abstract reference points such as the name of the service, specific environments, members of the support team and daily routines. For example, referring to 'Ashfield Crescent' and including a picture of the house was thought to be more meaningful than asking about 'your service'. Including a picture of someone's support team and asking them to name staff members ('John, Susan and Jeff') was preferable to simply asking about 'your support staff'. Interviewers could also make contextual references: in the communication and involvement questions interviewers and participants could look at the support folder, assess familiarity with the documents and talk about individual input. They could also talk about activities on a given day and discuss the level of choice-making an individual had been able to exercise.

The team devised a survey workspace which was printed onto sheets of A3 or A4 paper – with one sheet per question to minimise overwhelming participants. The workspace comprised a repeating format that allowed for familiarisation and fluency, but which could be individualised and adapted. The format comprised a three-part question structure: firstly an establishing statement that provided a concrete reference point; secondly a question that served as a prompt for discussion; thirdly a statement drawn from that question, with an adapted rating response that could then be scored according to a Likert scale.

All of these elements could be individualised. Some establishing statements used photographs of the service and staff team printed on the sheets, some used established symbols used in day-to-day choice-making, and others used writing. The rating scale, printed in a traffic-light colour scheme, was also adapted – some worksheets had 'thumbs up' or 'thumbs down' symbols where the person used these symbols in day-to-day expression, in other instances concrete answers were used (i.e. 'I decide' or 'staff decide' in questions about choice making). Participants used the workspace in different ways – some people moved cut-out photographs or symbol cards around the different spaces in the manner of the 'Talking Mats' technique as they worked the question through and arrived at a rating. Some people wrote or drew onto the sheets of paper, others engaged in purely verbal discussion.

Many practitioners reported that individuals had exceeded their expectations in participating and 30 survey interviews were completed across the organisation. Only one selected individual was unable to take part as they were undergoing a period of illness and associated stress. The survey process highlighted many positive areas of the organisation's work including high levels of well-being and positive relations with staff. The consultation also highlighted several areas for organisational improvement to which the management team are responding. These include promoting greater voice and involvement. For example, responses highlighted the need for greater involvement in producing service records and documents and accordingly the organisation is experimenting with portable technology and mixed media applications as a means of facilitating individual voice in records (see below). The survey also highlighted a need for greater involvement in recruitment processes and the organisation is increasingly using panels of supported people in recruitment and greater input into interview questions and staff requirement profiles – initiatives that have already been developed in some parts of the organisation. Systematic consultation can therefore lead to genuine changes in practice if thoroughly and meaningfully undertaken.

Voice and participation as a research focus

Voice and participation have been the focus of a research project undertaken within Scottish Autism's services. The project followed an action research model: seeking to ask critical questions of day-to-day support and to undertake case studies of practice in order to answer those questions (Elliot, 1991; Whitehead & McNiff, 2006). In doing so the team of practitioner-researchers that initiated the work have sought to harness the experiences and opinions of supported people, their families, and support practitioners.

The voice and participation project has sought to document and evaluate examples of effective individual and collective involvement in determining support and service provision[1]. We followed a number of initiatives that sought to achieve a greater level of involvement for supported people: mixed media service reviews; the use of mobile apps for choice-making; creative projects to recognise and validate individual voice; inclusive service meetings and school assemblies; and service forums and newsletters.

James, a participant in the case study on autistic-led newsletters summed up very well what he and others wanted to see from these initiatives:

James: *'I like the picture of Euan planting a tree because you don't see staff trying to guide. Someone's planting a tree but you don't see staff support. It's the first time I've seen a newsletter where there's no staff pictures, or staff training news. That's what I want to see.'*

Practitioner-researcher: *'Why do you think the newsletter is so important?'*

James: *'I like to see people discussing things instead of being bottled up. I think it's really important. I like people telling their stories without a single word of 'private and confidential', that's what I want to see. People able to speak.'*

James has since become a key contributor to service forums and to staff training.

One element of the project has been experimentation with different media to contribute to service reviews and records. These documents have traditionally been dominated by practitioner voices with writing as the main medium. It is still common practice in many social care services to have preferences and choices stated in the first person in the service records of less verbally articulate individuals, but in words written by service staff. The project team have instead sought to find ways of recognising and validating the voices and preferred means of communication of supported people, an approach greatly facilitated by the availability of digital and portable media.

David has experimented with using mobile technology to record his own self-updates for his support plan. David uses short phrases in his speech but has a keen interest in video and photography and records many of his activities on his own video camera. Practitioner-researchers have therefore harnessed this particular interest in order to support David to have a greater voice within his support records. With the use of a tablet computer and the 'Our Story' app, David has begun to record and photograph his favourite activities in order to document his experiences and express his preferences. Where practitioners initially curated David's videos and photographs with a written narrative and labels such as 'my walk in the park', the support team gradually moved to David recording his own labels in spoken form. Moreover, once he had learned to use the technology, David began to take control of the images to word his own labels, so that instead of a picture of David walking in the park, taken by staff, David chose to instead to take a picture of the grass verge. When asked to record a caption for this picture, David commented 'the long grass is dying', recalling the details that he had noticed in the environment there. In this way David provided a first-person view of the memory that he associated with the walk, rather than a simple labelling exercise or practitioner-led narrative.

The focus of these case studies has therefore been as much about practitioners learning where they can take a step back and foreground supported people's voices, as it has about autistic individuals learning new skills and processes. As such it has been important to record these contextual changes and mutual learning rather than simply focus on the capacities or skills of the supported autistic person. Preserving authenticity of individual voice has been a significant learning point from the project.

Another case study followed a young man, Paul, in creating his own visual timetable to structure days out in his local community. Paul had often been left to make decisions on the day about which activities he would like to do, something he struggled with without proper processing time. Paul was further frustrated when support staff or family sought to make decisions for him or change his activities at the last minute. Practitioner-researchers followed Paul's transition to creating his own visual timetable ahead of community days. The team harnessed Paul's growing computer skills so that he has learned to search for activities on the internet, place them on a document template himself, and print this out ahead of his community day. Paul then uses the document as a point of reference to remember and reinforce to others his chosen activities. In this way he has not only exercised greater choice, but ownership of the process of documenting and advocating these choices.

Paul also took a lead in how his case study was documented. Opting to have his sessions filmed at intervals, Paul took to showing the camera his process, demonstrating the elements of his timetable, and talking to researchers throughout. In this way Paul was able to communicate his process in a medium that he found meaningful. Where we sought to capture Paul's comments in documenting and presenting this case study we again opted for verbatim representation of dialogue to preserve the authenticity of voice:

Practitioner-researcher: *'Who do you show it to?'*

Paul: *'My family.'*

Researcher: *'And what do they say?'*

Paul: *'They say "that looks great, that looks fine."'*

Researcher: *'Do you keep it on a wall, on a desk?'*

Paul: *'I keep it on my desk.'*

Researcher: *'So what do you think about making this?'*

Paul: *'It's easy.'*

Researcher: *'It's easy? Do you think Wednesdays are better for having one of these?'*

Paul: *'Yeah, I like it. I like it like this. I like it.'*

The project team have presented this work at practitioner workshops within the organisation and co-presented and co-authored outputs with supported participants. The team have also produced an evidence-informed guide to voice

---

1 See Long *et al* (2017) for a more full account of this project, including some of the examples given here.

and participation drawing on the case studies that were undertaken. In this way the work has focused attention on the terminology of voice and participation within the organisation, started some important conversations between staff and the people they support, and underlined the ethical imperative to greater involvement of supported people in key decisions about their services.

Concluding remarks: an ongoing journey

Citizen participation is often conceptualised on a continuum: from practices that take place without consent through consultation, to co-creation and control. This was famously conceptualised by Arnstein as a progressive 'ladder of participation' (Arnstein, 1969). We would not claim that the initial projects within Scottish Autism's programme represent a model of complete control and remain aware of the power imbalances and inequalities that still exist in both research and practice. However, through introducing adapted methods of research engagement to facilitate individual voice; through focusing attention on meaningful involvement in support practice; and through initiating co-produced case studies and co-authored outputs, our first wave of projects has helped us to take some significant steps up this ladder. Moreover, these first efforts have shone a light on ways in which greater participation can be achieved. As we move forward with our programme, supported autistic people will be involved from the initial conception of projects throughout the research process – directing inquiry, and contributing as co-researchers and partners in better understanding the lived experience of support services.

Acknowledgements

We wish to acknowledge the many people involved in the work described here: the supported autistic people and consultants that collaborated on case studies and guided the survey work; the supported individuals, families and practitioners that participated in research; and the practitioner research and survey development teams.

References

Arnstein SR (1969) A ladder of citizen participation. *Journal of the American Institute of Planners* **35** (4) 216–224.

Association for Real Change (2015) *The Charter for Involvement. National Involvement Network & The Scottish Government*. Available at: (http://arcuk.org.uk/scotland/files/2011/09/ARC-final-charter-297mmx297mm-12.12.14.pdf (accessed September 2017).

Barnes C & Mercer G (2006) Independent futures. Creating user-led disability services in a disabling society. *Scandinavian Journal of Disability Research* **8** (4) 317–320.

Beresford P & Campbell J (1994) Disabled people, service users, user involvement and representation. *Disability & Society* **9** (3): 315–325.

Chown N, Robinson J, Beardon L, et al. (2017) Improving research about us, with us: a draft framework for inclusive autism research. *Disability & Society* **32** (5) 720–734.

Department of Health (2001) *Valuing People: A new strategy for learning disability for the 21st century*. DH: London.

Department of Health (2002) *Involving Patients and the Public in Health Care*. London: TSO.

Department of Health (2007) *Putting People First: A Shared Vision and Commitment to the Transformation of Adult Social Care*. DH: London.

Duffy S (2003) *Keys to citizenship: A guide to getting good support services for people with learning difficulties*. Paradigm Consultancy & Development Agency Limited.

Elliot J (1991) *Action Research For Educational Change*. Maidenhead, McGraw-Hill Education.

HM Government (2007) *The Local Government and Public Involvement Health Act*. London: TSO.

Long J, Panese J, Ferguson J, Hamill M & Miller J. (2017, in press) Enabling voice and participation in autism services: using practitioner research to develop inclusive practice. *Good Autism Practice* **18** (2).

Milton DE and Bracher M (2013) Autistics speak but are they heard? *Journal of the BSA MedSoc Group* **7** 61–69.

Murray D (2016) How to be equals, as required by the Care Quality Commission. In: D Milton & N Martin (Eds) *Autism and Intellectual Disability in Adults, Volume 1*. Brighton: Pavilion Publishing & Media.

Oliver M (1990) *The Politics of Disablement: A sociological approach*. New York: St. Martin's Press.

Pellicano L, Dinsmore A & Charman T (2013) *A Future Made Together: Shaping autism research in the UK*. London: Institute of Education.

The Scottish Government (2013) *The Keys to Life. Improving quality of life for people with learning disabilities*. Edinburgh: The Scottish Government.

Whitehead J & McNiff J (2006) *Action Research: Living theory*. London: SAGE Publications.

Knowing me – knowing me:

Changing the story around stigma and 'behaviours of concern'; promoting self-awareness, self-control and a positive narrative

Professor Richard Mills and Dr Michael McCreadie

Abstract

This short article describes an approach to working with people who are at risk or stigmatised by reason of 'behaviours of concern'. It was developed with our colleagues from the Laskaridis Foundation, Piraeus, Greece in response to a growing need for Greek schools to be more inclusive of children displaying 'challenging behaviours'. Our initial work was at a time when Greek schools were facing new challenges from accepting children who were refugees. Teachers were also facing great personal and professional hardships related to austerity. The approach therefore needed to be values-led, in that acceptance and respect were paramount. It had to be sensitive to local circumstances, culture and resources and the need to build local capacity to help children with highly diverse needs. This is a brief overview and discussion of the Synergy approach, and how this can be used to promote a well-being culture and a changed narrative across a range of education and social care services for people of all ages who may be at risk – not just those relating to autism.

Overview

The Synergy programme is a partnership between AT-Autism UK and the Laskaridis Foundation in Greece and was launched in 2014. It has now been accredited by the CPD accreditation programme. The model operates through a system of teacher support offered by local mentors and in turn supported by the team from AT-Autism.

Broadly, the approach is comprised of three main elements:

1. To be in control of oneself.
2. Deep understanding and sensitivity to narratives.
3. Listening, not judging, and the importance of role models.

These components are underpinned by evidence-supported practice derived from established psychological and physiological theory.

1. To be in control of oneself

Workers in education and human services frequently encounter people at risk of being stigmatised as a result of behaviours that create concern. The reasons for this are often difficult to understand and relate to factors beyond our control. Our own behaviour however is within our control and it is this that we focus on here.

Worker stress as a response to workplace events is not unique to human services. Other occupations face this but are arguably better at managing it. For example, airline pilots encounter high levels of personal stress on a daily basis as part of performing their professional role. They must be very highly trained in everything that can happen on a flight, so that in the event of an emergency there is a consistency of approach based on the best evidence of how to respond. This is not left to chance. It requires painstaking recruitment of would-be pilots, intensive preparation, training and rehearsal and evidence of competence before being passed fit to fly. Additionally, attention is paid to issues related to well-being and lifestyle, including rest and relaxation, workload and coping, and the physical environment. Contrast this with what we often find in human services, where the quality of recruitment, training, support and well-being are afforded lower priority and resources. Unlike pilots, workers in human services are routinely exposed to situations that are beyond their level of competence and experience. It is common practice to find the least experienced and least competent workers dealing with the most complex and stressful situations.

Can anything be done?

Even if desirable, interventions that change the behaviour of other human beings are elusive. This is evident from the host of unsuccessful approaches designed to change or manage human behaviour. Changing the behaviour of human beings by 'doing things to them' is incredibly difficult. On the other hand, an understanding of one's own behaviour and coping skills through guided self-reflection and self-awareness is not only

Knowing me – knowing me:

achievable but more likely to bring about positive and healthier outcomes for the worker and for the person receiving support. In all of this, an understanding of the impact of psychological and physiological factors at work is critical.

The natural response to dealing with crises, trauma or stressful events is instinctive and can best be summarised as 'flight or fight'. In this state the body is flooded with hormones that affect our thinking and the way we behave. The mind is highly alert and reacts impulsively. It is a natural reaction to danger. All human beings are programmed to behave this way. But although natural and important for survival, this reaction is also prone to errors and may create a sequence of events that can have undesirable, and in some cases disastrous, consequences. Examples of this might include the fairly innocuous, such as the panic experience of losing one's house keys or the more serious outcomes such as 'road rage' or a terrorist attack where an instinctive reaction can increase the danger. It is therefore problematic and training and rehearsal is needed to override it.

We now know that this natural reaction is also influenced by personal and cultural factors combined with conscious and unconscious biases. The psychologist Daniel Kahneman describes this instinctive process as the 'experiencing self', or 'system 1' (Kahneman, 2011).

Contrast this with a calmer and more reflective response where the pros and cons of a scenario are carefully evaluated leading to judgement and behaviour that is rational and deliberate. In this state the worker is in control of their own thoughts and importantly, the way they behave. Biases are challenged and discarded and a more authentic story is developed.

Being in touch with one's own emotions in this way is healthier and less likely to result in harmful stress. Kahneman describes this state as the 'thinking self', or 'system 2.' The task therefore is to move workers from 'experiencing and reacting' to 'thinking and responding' – from 'system 1' to 'system 2'.

This requires training in an approach that is not dissimilar to that designed for airline pilots – in that preparation and planning are vital, every eventuality is anticipated but recognised for what it is and free of bias. Dangers and hazards are not over or under estimated and rehearsal of responses ensures calm control over one's own actions at all times. It is about flicking an imaginary switch from 'experiencing self' to 'thinking self'.

A practical illustration of this concerns this example of 'road rage'. We gave the following scenario to a group of teachers. We asked what they made of it and what they would do.

Scenario

You are driving home. A blaring car horn startles you and you become aware of a car very close behind you repeatedly flashing its lights. A glance in the rear view mirror shows that car is being driven by a young male person wearing dark glasses, a reversed baseball cap and who is speaking on his mobile phone. He is dangerously close.

Our instinctive interpretation relies on a number of factors and will determine the response. First we may be startled – this produces a physiological reaction and causes us to go into flight or fight mode as the stress hormones kick in and rapid changes occur in our body. Based on our experience of young males we might then apply unconscious biases and interpret his behaviour as aggressive, which in turn causes us to 'fight' – by cursing him or other means – or less frequently by 'flight' – in this case avoidance.

In discussion we found people mostly reacted aggressively to this scenario – the 'fight' response. The narrative portrayed the driver and his behaviour as aggressive. People felt alarmed and upset by it. This was confirmed by personal and cultural biases associated with baseball caps, sunglasses and young males. The fact that he was also using a mobile phone merely served to confirm this narrative (confirmation bias) which interpreted his behaviour as aggression.

Various uncomplimentary terms were used to describe this driver such as 'madman' 'drunken crazy person', 'idiot', 'lunatic', 'a**hole', 'dangerous b**tard' and similar. Responses varied from 'I would give him the finger', 'I would brake hard so he had to swerve to avoid me', even 'I would pretend to brake by pressing the brake pedal to p*ss him off'. These are all examples of an instinctive 'experiencing self' or 'system 1' response.

We then gave additional information. This concerned what they were unable to see.

The young man's partner is on the back seat of the car in child birth. She is haemorrhaging. He is speaking to the hospital doctor who has advised him to get her to hospital within the next ten minutes otherwise he might lose her and the baby.

We asked if this changed things. Everyone felt it did. We had opened up the possibility of a different narrative where rather than a 'madman' the driver was a devoted husband and victim of tragic circumstances and where we were in the wrong by obstructing him.

The additional information allowed biases and stereotypes to be challenged along with the previously held explanation of his behaviour. This deeper understanding – of how we get in touch with the young man's experience – is referred to by sociologist Max Weber as *verstehen*, and is often missing from simplistic analysis of situations and behaviour that comprises only what we can see which will be further compounded by our conscious and unconscious biases (Weber, 1949).

As such, a deeper understanding is often incredibly difficult; we invited the teachers to consider a future where they would have a plan to ensure they remain in control come what may. They would be in control regardless of what other drivers might do and would remain calm and in control even if the cause of road rage *was* an aggressive act. To always 'think about what might be happening on the back seat of the car!'. In other words, the 'thinking self' or 'system 2'.

On follow up feedback was interesting. All reported a positive change in their coping ability and stress levels. One teacher told us that 'thinking things through' in this way helped her to remain calm and in control in other areas of her life and that she was also less irritated by her partner's annoying habits!

System 1 and system 2, or the experiencing self and thinking self, do not only apply to crises. Our values and behaviour are heavily influenced by the narrative that flows from the roles that we occupy and these in turn are linked to our biases and the way we interpret the world. How we are perceived and how we perceive others. This also relates to status and power and to expectations. In 1970 Goffman observed that in the institution an inmate who had resided there for many years was seen as subservient and of lower status than the newest most junior member of staff. 'Inmates' were intrinsically seen as less human and less important than 'staff'. This established an unspoken hierarchy and a narrative of 'them vs us' – now often referred to as 'othering'.

'Othering' is a term used to describe the way we treat people we regard as deviant or different and that difference is negatively perceived. For example in the case of immigrants or refugees, racist stereotypes have caused even government to behave in ways that would be unacceptable if applied to its own citizens. 'We' are not like 'them'.

This 'othering' also applies to children and adults with disabilities or cognitive differences such as those found in autism, or cognitive impairments as in those found in older people or those with dementia. In such circumstances the instinctive or experiencing self (system 1) tendency is to see the label, not the person. This results in stereotyped attitudes and behaviours that are depersonalising or stigmatising, even if well-meaning, which in turn produce a powerful and damaging narrative. Harsh, brutal or repressive regimes such as those found in some schools, care homes or prisons, or even kindly but patronising responses that restrict autonomy or human rights are all indicators of 'othering' caused by the integration of biases into belief systems and language. Reacting instinctively (the experiencing self-system 1) to people described as exhibiting 'challenging behaviour' typically stigmatises such individuals and evokes fearful or aggressive reactions and creates a narrative of low expectations where neglect or abuse is permissible or tolerated.

Alternatively, getting to know and understand 'the person as a person' and building an alternative story around them is the thinking self – system 2. This offers protection on a number of levels to the worker and the person receiving support and is broadly in two parts.

Firstly, our thinking state is mindful and watchful. Alert to the dangers of how we are affected by conscious and unconscious bias and our altered physiology and psychological responses to stress. In this we are always working to begin our day and to remain in control of ourselves; to be calm, kind, respectful and rational. This demands training and practice. There are exercises to promote and develop this.

Secondly, our responses are planned, thorough and thought through. Some are positive such as insisting on respectful, inclusive outlook and behaviour from colleagues. Or negative as in preventing harmful practice e.g. not allowing inexperienced or ill-equipped colleagues to take on tasks beyond them. We plan and prepare. We rehearse. We think. We are imaginative and curious but always in control of ourselves and alert to factors that could drag us unwittingly into system 1.

Based on our experience of education and human services, we suggest that services and workers are too often operating in experiencing self where they are for at least part of their time physiologically and psychologically not in control. This is likely to be compounded by a host of personal, institutional and cultural factors and of conscious and unconscious biases. These combine to produce the harmful behaviour and narratives evidenced by the many scandals involving human services over the years.

2. Deep understanding and sensitivity to narratives

Weber described 'verstehen' as a means of deep understanding that encapsulated a multitude of factors, not least the experience of the other. The scientific practice of testing only that which can be defined in scientific terms is disputed. In this way simplistic or reductive explanations of human behaviour such as crude behaviourist or medical models are rejected. Human behaviour is multifaceted and as we have demonstrated, based as much on the unseen, such as thoughts, feelings and beliefs, as it is on what is observable. ABC charts or psychotropic medications are not adequate replacements for trying to experience the world from the perspective of the other person. Taking the time to do this also addresses one of the main areas of concern in this field; labelling those behaviours we do not understand as 'psychotic', 'autistic' or 'complex' or medicating or restraining people on the basis of institutional, cultural or personal biases.

As has been argued earlier, the development of stories, or narratives around groups and individuals, is highly significant in both practice and policy. For example, in the UK, it was only in the 1970's that children with intellectual disabilities were deemed entitled to education. Previously regarded as uneducable, such children either remained at home with parents or went to an occupation centre. Schools were not provided as they were deemed unnecessary as 'these' children could not be educated. The narrative of 'low potential' became a self-fulfilling prophesy with low expectations leading to fewer resources leading to lower achievement.

In a similar vein focusing on one aspect of the person – such as specific behaviours of concern, their diagnosis, past history or reputation, colludes with our biases and the narrative to produce a perception and classification of 'dangerousness'. Thereafter everything about the person is viewed through this lens. Research has shown that merely labelling a person as A or B will determine the ongoing narrative, nature of any 'treatment' and outcome. Wolfensberger's essays on the importance of valued social roles for people at risk of stigmatisation remain as relevant today as ever, particularly when people may have more than one label attached to them (Wolfensberger, 1983). In 1974, Rosenhan found that simply labelling a sane person 'mentally ill' in a psychiatric hospital caused all of their behaviour to be viewed through the lens of mental illness. The current controversy around indeterminate prison sentences for people deemed dangerous is a further example of how such a narrative can trap all parties concerned.

3. Listening not judging and the importance of role models

Giving advice is easy – listening is hard. Psychologist Carl Rogers suggests that when faced with a problem, especially a crisis, it is usually easier and quicker to produce a ready-made solution than it is to listen (Rogers, 1959). But by failing to listen we not only risk disempowering others, we also unwittingly disconnect them from their own self-support system that enables them to think through and create their own solutions. We interfere with the self-reflection that is critical to developing self-sustaining coping strategies that underpin well-being and resilience. We promote dependency. We regard this as an important ethical issue.

Of course, people will often demand advice based on 'do this' or 'do that'; this is easier to deliver and requires little thinking about, but in practice is invariably little more than a re-hashing of selective memories of past incidents and accompanying biases. Moreover, many of these memories may, as a result of selective bias, also turn out to be false with 'successes' exaggerated and difficulties minimised. 'Why do you think this is happening?' is often a more effective response than 'I once knew a child that did that – you should do this'.

An approach that sees guided exploration through active listening and sensitive probing or 'Socratic' questioning, offers the most reliable means of developing ownership of solutions to problems. One where the worker develops a coping strategy based on deeper understanding of their own biases, strengths, weaknesses and capacity. Where they learn to manage these along with their personal stress, rather than merely perform a set of pre-determined instructions, such as part of a 'behaviour plan'. Such an approach will naturally include the person receiving support.

It may be that some schools and human services are already doing this but in our practice we have found few. Workers in such professions need support and effective leadership. Psychologist Albert Bandura argues that behavioural change and self-efficacy is more likely to be influenced by role models – for good and ill. We have seen examples of this from scandals; of how easily neglect or brutality is copied and becomes part of the institutional culture. But Vanier showed that it is also possible to influence culture by modelling acceptance, tolerance, kindness and thoughtfulness and found that worker well-being improved under these conditions (Vanier, 2013). Demonstrating humane and mindful practice whilst remaining calm, listening, and gently questioning are key leadership attributes and should be high on the 'essential list' for anyone fulfilling such a role in human services.

With its focus on the mind-set of the worker and not the behaviour of the person receiving support, we believe this approach has the potential to transform practice. Just as airlines require you to put on your own oxygen mask before helping others, the approach seeks to reduce stress and develop the capacity and resilience in the worker as a means of helping others.

We continue to do our best and develop Synergy alongside our colleagues, mindful of our need to reflect and to be vigilant in the light of our experiences and biases – both conscious and unconscious.

For more information on the Synergy programme contact the authors richardmills@atautism.org, michaelmccreadie@atautism.org or info@atautism.org

References

Kahneman D (2011) *Thinking, Fast and Slow*. New York: Farrar, Straus and Giroux.

Rogers CR (1959) *A Theory of Therapy, Personality, and Interpersonal Relationships: As developed in the client-centered framework (Volume 3)*. New York: McGraw-Hill.

Vanier J (2013). *The Heart of L'Arche: A spirituality for every day*. London: SPCK Publishing.

Weber M (1949) *Methodology of Social Sciences*. The Free Press.

Wolfensberger W (1983) Social role valorization: a proposed new term for the principle of normalization. *Mental Retardation* **21** (6) 234.

Further reading

Bandura A (1977) *Social Learning Theory*. New Jersey: Prentice-Hall Inc.

Bandura A (1982) Self-efficacy mechanism in human agency. *American Psychologist* **37** (2) 122.

Bubb S (2014) *Winterbourne View – Time for Change: Transforming the commissioning of services for people with learning disabilities and/or autism*. London: NHS England.

Dunne J (1986) Sense of community in l'Arche and in the writings of Jean Vanier. *Journal of Community Psychology* **14** (1) 41–54.

Eaton WW (1994) Social facts and the sociological imagination: the contributions of sociology to psychiatric epidemiology. *Acta Psychiatrica Scandinavica* **90** (s385) 25–38.

Goffman E (1961) *Asylums: Essays on the social situation of mental patients and other inmates*. New York: Anchor Books.

McDonnell A, McCreadie M, Mills R, Deveau R, Anker R & Hayden J (2015) The role of physiological arousal in the management of challenging behaviours in individuals with autistic spectrum disorders. *Research in developmental disabilities* **36** 311–322.

Milton DE (2012) On the ontological status of autism: the 'double empathy problem'. *Disability & Society* **27** (6) 883–887.

Milton D, Mills R & Pellicano L (2012) Ethics and autism: where is the autistic voice? Commentary on Post et al. *Journal of autism and developmental disorders* **44** (10) 2650–2651.

Palys TS (2003) *Research decisions: Quantitative and qualitative perspectives*. Scarborough, OT: Thomson Nelson.

Rogers C (1995) *A Way of Being*. Boston: Houghton Mifflin Harcourt.

Rosenhan DL (1974) On being sane in insane places. *Clinical Social Work Journal* **2** (4) 237–256.

Rosenstock IM, Strecher VJ & Becker MH (1988) Social learning theory and the health belief model. *Health Education Quarterly* **15** (2) 175–183.

Scheff TJ (1970) *Being Mentally ill: A sociological theory*. Didcot: Transaction Publishers.

Sherif CW, Sherif M & Nebergall RE (1981) *Attitude and Attitude Change: The social judgment-involvement approach*. Westport, CT: Greenwood Press.

Sherif M (1998) Experiments in group conflict. In: JM Jenkins and K Oatley (Eds) *Human Emotions: A reader* (pp245-252). Malden, MA: Blackwell.

Schwitzgebel E (2006) Belief. In: E Zalta (Ed.) *The Stanford Encyclopedia Of Philosophy*. Stanford University.

Smith JK (1983) Quantitative versus qualitative research: an attempt to clarify the issue. *Educational Researcher* **12** (3) 6–13.

Traustadóttir R (2009, May) Disability studies, the social model and legal developments. In: *The UN Convention on the Rights of Persons with Disabilities* (pp1–16). Brill.

Tucker WT (1965) Max Weber's Verstehen. *The Sociological Quarterly* **6** (2) 157–164.

Tversky A & Kahneman D (1973) Availability: a heuristic for judging frequency and probability. *Cognitive Psychology* **5** (2) 207–232.

Tversky A & Kahneman D (1975) Judgment under uncertainty: Heuristics and biases. In: D Wendt & C Vlek (Eds) *Utility, Probability, and Human Decision Making* (pp141–162). Netherlands: Springer Nature.

Section 3:
From theory to practice

Considering employment of young people with intellectual impairment and autism leaving school and college

Chris Barnham and Professor Nicola Martin

Abstract

This article begins by exploring relevant UK legislation and government initiatives designed to support transition to work for young disabled people, and reflects upon their relevance, specifically for autistic individuals with additional intellectual impairments. Research from within and beyond the UK has painted a positive picture of the benefit of employment to the employee and the workplace, whilst noting that systems to support and encourage engagement with work are somewhat patchy and often underdeveloped.

The series of illustrative vignettes in the second part of this chapter have been created to illustrate some of the strengths autistic people might bring to work, along with some of the barriers which may need to be addressed in order to help individuals to flourish. We conclude with a few practical recommendations. The systematic provision of opportunities to try out real-life work situations in order to make informed choices is highly recommended, particularly for people who find it hard to imagine situations they have not experienced before. Job trials are likely to be preferable to interviews, and adequately trained and supervised work place mentors may well have a role to play. Ensuring that people who find it difficult to communicate verbally are enabled to make their ideas known is identified as an important consideration. Obviously clear, transparent and easy access to systems like 'Access to Work' would be helpful.

Introduction and scope

The aim of this chapter is to stimulate discussion about practical ways in which employers and practitioners from various disciplines might help young autistic people (who also have intellectual impairments) to transition from education to employment, and to flourish in the workplace. Austerity concerns and interactions between the benefits system and employment of disabled people fall outside the scope of this paper. At the time of writing the 2017 UK general election has just occurred and resulted in a (minority) Conservative government. We think it's fair to say that the future is uncertain. Documenting historic concerns is probably pointless as this chapter is looking forward to consider practical ways in which work could be made more accessible to young autistic people with intellectual impairments. Barnham (2016) reflects on the disability employment gap, and the initiatives of the previous Conservative (majority) government, which arguably had little positive employment impact for the group with which we are concerned. This chapter is not looking outside the UK particularly, but it is interesting that scholars such as Hedley et al (2016) and Wehman et al (2016; 2017) paint a similar picture in their studies focusing on Australia and America. These studies illustrated both the value of employment and the lack of systematic support for securing and maintaining a job. It is possible that we will now be looking in the UK towards a new set of interventions and we live in hope that these are to be practical, beneficial and informed by the ideas and concerns of autistic people.

Previous initiatives

Some historic attempts to address the under employment of disabled people in general, and autistic people in particular, have a degree of relevance to our discussion. Information is included in the next section to provide some context, which may stimulate thinking about what might be usefully developed and taken forward. Research Autism (http://www.researchautism.net/autism-publications/literature-reviews-autism/vocational-reviews-autism) provides a list of some useful autism-focused articles.

16-25 education

The Children and Families Act (CFA) (2014) requires colleges and other post-16 providers to offer students study programmes which are coherent, appropriately challenging, and designed to support progression to apprenticeship or employment. This requirement covers 16-25 year olds where they have either a statement of special educational needs (SEN) or an education and health care plan (EHCP).

Students with autism and intellectual impairment within this age range would fall under this umbrella and none of the political manifestos recently published suggest radical reforms of the CFA. Further education (FE) is not currently faring well in funding terms. FE providers receive learning support funding, to help them support learners with learning difficulties and disabilities by meeting the costs of reasonable adjustments, as recommended in the Children and Families Act (2014) and congruent with the ethos of the Equality Act (2010). Many disabled students receive information, advice and guidance on employment/career choice, CV writing and volunteering opportunities. Some have access to work-focused coaches and mentors, but these schemes are few and far between and often fall short of the ideal standard of mentor training and supervision (Milton et al, 2017). A systematic review conducted by Gibson et al (2017) highlighted the obvious importance of hands-on, systematic, high-quality, well-organised work experience for students with intellectual impairments transitioning from education to employment.

Current initiatives

Current study programmes with a strong employment focus include the following. The relevant websites for these can be found in the resources list at the end of the chapter.

Supported internships

These are unpaid, structured study programmes, based primarily with employers, which aim to help young people aged 16-24 (who have EHC plans or statements of SEN) to achieve sustainable paid employment through developing the skills they need for work by learning these skills in the workplace. For autistic learners, developing skills in context has potential advantages, or at least may reduce the requirement to generalise from simulated classroom-based learning into the real workplace. Supported internships were trialed in 2012/13 in 15 FE colleges. Evaluation published in December 2013 found that 36 percent resulted in paid employment (Department for Education, 2013). The unpaid nature of these initiatives is obviously a cause for some equity concerns.

Traineeships

These aim to help young people who want to get an apprenticeship or job but do not yet have appropriate skills or experience. Traineeships are based on a mainstream education and training programme, with work experience focused on the sort of skills and experience that employers seek. At the core is work preparation training, English and maths for those that need it, and a high quality work placement. Where the emphasis is placed on English and maths mastery, a barrier can potentially arise for some people aspiring to a traineeship.

Apprenticeships

These were described as a priority for Theresa May's majority government which introduced the 'apprenticeship levy' (HM Revenue & Customs, 2016). They are designed to allow young people or adult learners to earn while they learn in a real job, whilst also gaining a qualification. May's pre-June 2017 government showed signs of commitment to making apprenticeships inclusive and accessible and incentivising employers to embrace the idea of offering them. An understanding of the requirements of potential apprentices who have autism and intellectual impairment would clearly be essential in order for this group to benefit and for employers to make the most of the potential value those with the skill sets often associated with autism might bring to work. Where maths and English qualification requirements are stipulated, further obstacles can occur.

A number of labour market programmes presently exist to offer help to people with learning difficulties and disabilities, including:

Work Choice

This is a voluntary programme which is described as offering disabled people a range of help to find, get and thrive in a job. Over a quarter of Work Choice referrals (27 percent) have learning disability recorded as their primary impairment.

Access to Work

Access to Work provides grants to cover additional costs of starting or staying in work (including traineeships and supported internships). This can include specialist equipment, transport costs, support or workplace job coaching and disability awareness training for colleagues. 36,470 people used Access to Work in 2015/16 (Department for Work & Pensions, 2016). The need for job coaches to understand, without stereotyping, the sort of challenges and strengths someone with autism and intellectual impairment might bring, has already been stated. Disability awareness training reflecting the voices of autistic people would be ideal.

Disability employment advisers

The Department for Work & Pensions has a network of around 400 Disability Employment Advisers in Job Centres. Part of their remit is to understand the various initiatives described here, including Access to Work. Autistic people could usefully find employment delivering their training.

Disability Confident campaign

This campaign is an initiative through which May's last government worked with employers with the aim of helping them feel more confident about employing disabled people through signposting available support and showcasing success stories. While 79 percent of employers said they 'would consider in principle' employing disabled people, only 22 percent had in the preceding 12 months. The gap between disabled and non-disabled employment rates varies widely by locality. A 2012 survey found that across the UK it was then 38 percent. In Cumbria it was 48 percent, while in Hertfordshire it was 25 percent (Office for National Statistics, 2012). Figures tended not to isolate information about people with autism and intellectual impairment so are of limited value to our discussion here. Success stories delivered by autistic people would help employers to see the benefits of creating work environments to support maximising the strengths of autistic workers.

Barriers to autistic young people with additional intellectual impairments entering and sustaining employment

This section discusses issues which focus more specifically on 'the group' under consideration (whilst always acknowledging the individuality of every person). Lack of flexibility in education may lead some learners to drop out or to leave education without the sort of qualifications which mean something to employers. This is particularly so for special school pupils who may not necessarily have access to qualifications they are capable of gaining. Douglas et al (2016) Potential obstacles relating to maths and English qualifications have already been discussed in relation to apprenticships and traineeships.

Disabled people may be reluctant to disclose to potential employers, fearing their abilities may be doubted before they get chance to demonstrate what they can do. Autistic people live with negative stereotypes, such as from the film *Rain Man* and this may well impact on decisions around 'disclosure' (which is, in itself, like 'disorder', a problematic D word).

Employers may look at what they perceive that a young disabled person *can't* do, rather than what they *can* do. When an individual with autism and intellectual impairment does not use their voice to communicate, the employer might make assumptions about their capabilities which are misjudged. Advocacy and self-advocacy may be required in order for this barrier to be addressed. In the case of advocacy, it is important that the advocate is on the same page as their 'client' and has achieved this by going to great lengths to find out what it is that the young person aspires to. Self-advocacy is only possible if the individual has been able to develop or has been equipped with a means of communication and has had access to a range of experiences which would enable them to make realistic choices. Mentoring under these circumstances is a highly skilled process requiring subtle, focused training and ongoing supervision.

Limited awareness amongst professionals of what support services are available for disabled young people create further blocks in the road to work. The elephant-sized roadblock is the lack of opportunities which are autism focused, autism informed and of high quality. Excellent opportunities for young people with autism and intellectual impairments are uncommon in the workplace, and poorly organized transitions can disrupt effective support.

There may be some system issues to consider. The Children and Families Act (2014) was underpinned by a philosophy of joined up thinking but it is not clear whether the responsibilities of schools, colleges, local authorities and government agencies are clear and complementary in relation to progression into work. Effective transitions for individuals need to be seamlessly supported, as change is already known to be challenging for autistic people, without introducing elements of avoidable chaos at a systems level. It is necessary to consider ways in which the process of assessment and securing support could be simplified, and made more 'transition-proof' as people move from education into work.

It is important to ascertain whether there is a consistent approach across government and sector. With a reliance on local authorities in the school years and individual institutions and providers of FE, and a range of initiatives (examples of which were provided earlier) to support progression to work, the sense of there being a joined up approach is tenuous. The extent to which information, advice and guidance is autism aware, autism informed, readily available to autistic people, and able to support autistic people (including those with intellectual impairments) in tackling barriers to work, is unquantified. Although the Equality Act (2010) exists and the Children and Families Act is specifically targeted at smoothing the 16-24 transition, there isn't a clear sense of a national picture around good practice in, for example, disclosing to employers, seeking reasonable adjustments and accessing support such as Access to Work. The Autism Act (2009) and subsequent Adult Autism Strategy (Department of Health, 2015) were designed to improve 'the local offer' and to up-skill the workforce of public servants who may impact on the lives of autistic people, but this has not translated into an army of autism-aware people willing and able to help their autistic clients to find and keep a job. Company human resource departments may well be on the front-line when it comes to the employability equality agenda but there is scant evidence of autism-focused, autism-informed training to help personnel in these roles to be effective.

Possible solutions – first thoughts

Barnham's 2016 report posed some questions which related to the wider community of potential disabled employees but also resonate here. The report was written prior to the 2017 general election being called and this chapter has been authored while the minority Conservative government is still settling. We live in hope that, whichever party is in power in the future, autistic voices will influence the trajectory of any reforms and that these will be sensible and adequately resourced. For a detailed exploration of government policies and initiatives relating to the employment of autistic people see also Parkin (2016).

Barnham (2016) proposed that in view of the focus on 0-25 in special educational needs and disability, further education and employers may be best placed to work with the grain of that change toward employment outcomes. For those who use means other than verbal language as their main mode of communication, there may be mileage in some kind of 'passport', which could outline strengths and support requirements to ease the transition to work. Case studies from employers could possibly be used to develop a 'transition toolkit' and training materials aimed at potential employers and gatekeepers to employment (such as job centre staff).

Autism and intellectual impairment focus: hypothetical case studies and discussion

Mentoring

The Research Autism Cygnet Mentoring project based at London South Bank University (Milton et al, 2016) highlighted the benefits of goal orientated fixed term mentoring to enable autistic adults to identify and achieve their own goals, including goals around employment. While the focus of the project did not specifically encompass the requirements of people with autism and additional intellectual impairments, the lessons learned are pertinent. Issues of cognition and communication require careful consideration in relation, particularly, to addressing the requirements of people who may not communicate well verbally and may have difficulty

Illustrative vignettes

Anna

Anna attends a special school. She is seventeen years old, communicates with the aid of visual supports (pictures) and can make choices between two pictures or two objects, with understanding. She has strong likes and dislikes and it is easy enough for people who know Anna to work out what these are because her nonverbal communication is effective. Her preference is to be outside. Anna's school is organizing work experience and this has been discussed with her, using picture aids. When given a picture of a car and a picture of a greenhouse and asked 'which one do you like', she pointed to the greenhouse. The work experience will be in a garden centre greenhouse. Anna will be supported by a teaching assistant and will plant bedding plants for two hours a day over a one week period. When Anna gets to the garden centre she is distressed as she does not like the feel of the soil on her hands. The work placement is not a success.

Anna really likes being in the park. At eighteen years old she spent three hours a day, two days a week over four weeks with her teaching assistant and a park worker, and was able to see and try out various tasks including planting, sweeping and picking up litter. Anna indicated a preference for picking up litter and had a very successful work experience in the park after it had been established that she would be litter picking.

After Anna left school at nineteen years old she was supported in developing a portfolio of activities including continuing her education at a further education college and focusing on independent living and employability skills. By twenty-one Anna was living in supported accommodation with two other young women and with some support was working two days a week picking up litter and working in the greenhouse in the park. On a further two days each week she was accessing the community with assistance. This included going to the cinema on a Tuesday afternoon. Anna was able to communicate her choices and had a weekly timetable with pictures and symbols to help her to make sense of her activities. As she is not yet twenty-five, her Education and Health Care Plan still operates as a coordinating document between the various agencies working together to help Anna to reach her potential.

The following three examples from The Cygnet Project mentor training (Milton et al, 2017) further illustrate some of the sorts of issues which might arise at work and the requirement for sensitivity and clarity on the part of the mentor.

Ali

Ali is a very hard worker who loves everything to do with gardening. He does not mind the weather, is always punctual and extremely reliable. When he is given detailed instructions, sometimes with a sequence of pictures to help him if a task is unfamiliar, he just gets on with it. Recently he has been exploited by a peer who has passed his work onto Ali and sat in the shed on his phone. Ali does not realise that his mate is exploiting his good nature. This situation will not change unless someone very sensitive intervenes in a way which does not ruin Ali's enjoyment of his job.

Jean

Jean is reliable, serious, hardworking and productive. She has recently started a clerical job in an open plan office which is hot, noisy, crowded and has strip lighting. Her bus was late, she stood up all the way and arrived late. Her supervisor said 'what time do you call this'. Jean looked flustered and the supervisor said 'never mind, just finish that stuff off from Friday, chop chop'. Jean went to the toilet and locked herself in.

Jean is still in the toilet after half an hour. She is sitting on the floor, feeling hot, anxious and frightened. She is very quiet and preoccupied and is not sure how to get herself out of the situation. Her supervisor is asking office staff where she is. Jean can hear him. Jean's workplace mentor arrives and is told what is going on by the supervisor. The mentor takes it from there.

Simon

Simon attends an FE college and his course includes a work placement one day a week as a car valet. He has been coached into the role by a volunteer job coach, Abdul, who works at the car valeting workshop full time. Abdul was supported to understand Simon's requirements in order to assist him effectively. Simon does not use speech and a communication passport was developed as the main tool to initially get across Simon's likes, dislikes, strengths and general way of operating. He is good at imitating and Abdul is good at demonstrating. In the first few weeks Abdul would demonstrate a task, such as polishing, and Simon would copy. The order of tasks was always logical and sequential. By week 5 Abdul and Simon worked side-by-side on separate cars. Abdul keeps an eye on Simon and both of them enjoy the experience of working together. Abdul has access to a supervisor from the college in case he has any questions and Simon's work experience is also monitored by college staff.

with the concept of 'future self'. This idea was discussed fully by Sally Brett in the first volume of this series and Sally's article merits a second read (Brett, 2016).

Mentoring people with autism and intellectual impairments towards thinking about employment requires the mentor to avoid a tokenistic and bossy engagement with the complex question of what an individual might like to do as a job in the future, particularly when ideas like 'job' and 'future' are not something which is easily comprehensible. Concepts which may seem quite abstract need to be made meaningful for an individual via the provision of opportunities for lived experience. Saying 'would you like to work in horticulture?' within a sterile indoor environment will certainly make far less sense to someone who does not know what 'working in horticulture' involves, than would the opportunity to get their hands dirty in the act of planting seeds or bedding plants.

The Cygnet project used fictional vignettes to illustrate the sort of mentoring which may be effective in the workplace and these were incorporated into mentor training. Autistic voices were prominent in all mentor training sessions and this was commented on by participants as a real strength. For Cygnet, resources like the channel 'silentmiaow' on YouTube (https://www.youtube.com/user/silentmiaow) (an autoethnographic account by an autistic person who does not communicate verbally but can explain her motivation using technology) helped with understanding nonverbal engagement with the world.

Further mentor training is being developed to specifically address the requirements of people who possibly have less understanding of employment or less capacity to express themselves conventionally with words than that of the Cygnet participants. This training will incorporate the concept of future self and the requirement to experience, in real life, what a job might be like, rather than to discuss it in an abstract context, even if this is with the aid of some form of visual prompt. A picture of a flowerpot does not convey the smell of compost.

Mentoring involves listening and helping the mentee to identify and work towards their own goals. When words are not the primary mode of communication, and concepts cannot be grasped easily in the abstract, the task of mentoring has to be approached differently. A more nuanced engagement is necessary to present ideas in a way in which the mentee will understand, often through access to real experience, and to ascertain the meaning the mentee is making of them. Listening can become watching the reaction of an individual within real contexts, which can convey more meaning than would be possible by looking at a two dimensional image. In an attempt to get this idea across in training, the following fictional stories have been devised.

Practical considerations

Work experience is important. It is particularly difficult for someone on the spectrum to imagine a situation which they have not experienced, therefore exposure to job taster opportunities is essential in order to facilitate informed choice. In the case study utilised as an example here, Simon very much enjoys his work experience in the car valeting shop.

Work trials with support are more appropriate than conventional interviews. Ali, for example, could shine in the greenhouse because of his enthusiasm for horticulture, but does not have the communications skills to get this across verbally. Anna didn't actually like planting things when she got to experience this in real life.

A work-placed mentor who understands the requirements of the individual would be helpful, at least initially, and on an ongoing basis as someone to turn to if difficulties arise. The requirements of the job role need to be explicitly communicated in ways which meet the requirements of the individual. Visual timetables, picture prompts and assistive technology have been discussed in the first volume of this series and are equally relevant at work. Help to navigate the social and sensory world of work will also be important. Jean is clearly finding the sensory environment of her office horrible. Anna had sensory issues with the feel of wet soil.

The chapter on Universal Design in the first volume of this publication (Milton *et al*, 2016) discusses strategies which would work in employment. The REAL model (Hastwell *et al*, 2013) for example, emphasises the requirement for reliability, clarity, anticipation (in order to avoid potential difficulties) and logical clear communication is readily applicable to work. Unclear communication is also having a negative impact on Jean. Anna could not make any sort of decision about the sort of work she might like when shown a picture of a car and a picture of a greenhouse. It is quite a big cognitive leap to make assumptions from these images to the real working world of horticulture or car maintenance.

Full, part time or voluntary employment can have a positive impact on well-being and self-esteem. Work which relates to the interests of the individual will be most rewarding. Simon loves cleaning cars and he is good at it. It is necessary to be imaginative about the sort of occupation that might be feasible with a little support, and to find ways of accessing an understanding of what the individual might like to do, especially if their mode of communication is unconventional. Observing that someone is happiest outside, for example, might lead down the path of looking at the feasibility of some sort of outdoor work. Anna's work involves being outside, which she likes, and is part of a portfolio of coordinated and fulfilling activities which make up a full and active timetable.

Background has been provided on funding streams such as Access to Work but there is evidence that these sources of support are poorly understood (Milton *et al*, 2017). The role of work-based volunteers also merits consideration, with caution. As with mentoring relationships, boundaries have to be clear, and supervision is important. Abdul is gaining a lot from his role in supporting Simon at work. He received adequate training to fulfil the role and knows that he has access to a supervisor. The sustainability of the arrangement merits discussion. Simon is on a college-based work placement but he is capable of making an ongoing contribution to the workplace with the right sort of support.

Conclusion

In a time of huge political uncertainty this paper has explored some of the issues which surround the idea of employment of autistic people with intellectual impairments. In an ideal world, gatekeepers would be committed to the idea and would know exactly what they are doing, having been trained by autistic people to understand the strengths and aspirations of autistic people, including those with intellectual impairments who do not use verbal language to communicate. In an ideal world work place mentors would be trained by autistic people and mentoring schemes would all be safely supervised. In an ideal world employers would welcome autistic people with intellectual impairments with open arms. In an ideal world joined up, adequately resourced, carefully monitored systems would smooth transitions and provide safe ongoing support to enable people with autism and intellectual impairments to flourish, not only in work, but in all aspects of their lives.

References

Barnham C (2016) *Through Learning to Earning: Final report of the transitions to employment sub-group, May 2016* [online]. Available at: http://businessdisabilityforum.org.uk/media-centre/newsletter/archive/2016/june-2016/new-report-recommends-action-on-transitions-into-employment-for-disabled-learners/ (accessed September 2017).

Brett S (2016) Future selves: Listening carefully to the voice of a KS5 pupil in a special school. In: D Milton and N Martin (Eds) *Autism and Intellectual Disability in Adults, Volume 1* (pp55–59). Hove: Pavilion Publishing and Media Ltd.

Department for Education (2013) *Learning Difficulties/disabilities: Supported internship evaluation* [online]. Available at: https://www.gov.uk/government/publications/learning-difficultiesdisabilities-supported-internship-evaluation (accessed September 2017).

Department of Health (2015) *Adult Autism Strategy: Statutory guidance* [online]. Available at: https://www.gov.uk/government/publications/adult-autism-strategy-statutory-guidance (accessed September 2017).

Department for Work & Pensions (2016) *Access to Work: Official statistics* [online]. Available at: https://www.gov.uk/government/uploads/system/uploads/attachment_data/file/538443/access-to-work-statistics-march-2016.pdf (accessed September 2017).

Douglas G, McLinden M, Robertson C, Travers J & Smith E (2016) Including pupils with special educational needs and disability in national assessment: comparison of three country case studies through an inclusive assessment framework. *International Journal of Disability, Development and Education*, **63** (1) 98–121.

Gilson CB, Carter EW & Biggs EE (2017) Systematic review of instructional methods to teach employment skills to secondary students with intellectual and developmental disabilities. *Research and Practice for Persons with Severe Disabilities*, **42** (2) 89–107.

Hastwell J, Harding J, Martin N & Baron-Cohen S (2013) *Asperger Syndrome Student Project, 2009-12, Final Report* [online]. University of Cambridge Disability Resource Centre. Available at: http://www.admin.cam.ac.uk/univ/disability/asperger/ASProjectReport2013.pdf (accessed September 2017).

Hedley D, Uljarević M, Cameron L, Halder S, Richdale A & Dissanayake C (2016) Employment programmes and interventions targeting adults with autism spectrum disorder: A systematic review of the literature. *Autism*, p.1362361316661855.

HM Revenue & Customs (2016) *Policy Paper: Apprenticeship levy* [online] https://www.gov.uk/government/publications/apprenticeship-levy/apprenticeship-levy (accessed September 2017).

Milton D, Martin M & Melham P (2016) Beyond reasonable adjustment: autistic-friendly spaces and Universal Design. In: D Milton and N Martin (Eds) *Autism and Intellectual Disability in Adults, Volume 1* (pp81–86). Brighton: Pavilion Publishing and Media Ltd.

Milton D, Sims T, Dawkins G, Martin N & Mills R (2017) The development and evaluation of a mentor training programme for those working with autistic adults. *Good Autism Practice* **18** (1) 25–33.

Parkin E (2016) *Autism: Overview of UK policy and services* [online]. Commons briefing papers CBP-7172. Available at: http://researchbriefings.parliament.uk/ResearchBriefing/Summary/CBP-7172#fullreport (accessed September 2017).

Wehman P, Brooke V, Brooke AM, Ham W, Schall C, McDonough J, Lau S, Seward H & Avellone L (2016) Employment for adults with autism spectrum disorders: a retrospective review of a customized employment approach. *Research in Developmental Disabilities* **53-54** 61–72.

Wehman P, Schall CM, McDonough J, Graham C, Brooke V, Riehle JE, Brooke A, Ham W, Lau S, Allen J & Avellone L (2017) Effects of an employer-based intervention on employment outcomes for youth with significant support needs due to autism. *Autism* **21** (3) 276–290.

Resources – initiatives

→ **Supported internships**
www.preparingforadulthood.org.uk/what-we-do/supported-internships

→ **Traineeships**
https://www.gov.uk/find-traineeship

→ **Apprenticeships**
https://www.gov.uk/government/publications/help-and-support-for-young-disabled-people-to-find-and-stay-in-work (guidance updated 27-06-17).

→ **Work Choice**
https://www.gov.uk/work-choice/overview

→ **Access to Work**
https://www.gov.uk/access-to-work/overview

→ **Disability Employment Advisers**
www.jobcentreguide.co.uk/jobcentre-plus-guide/34/disability-employment-advisors

→ **Disability Confident campaign**
https://www.gov.uk/government/collections/disability-confident-campaign

Employment: a reflective review

Dr Damian EM Milton

Abstract

This chapter explores the employment of autistic people via an 'aut-ethnographic' case-study approach (Milton, 2014a) to the issue of starting a new job, with particular regard as to what can be learnt from such a personal story in the context of mentoring young autistic adults beginning a period of employment. A number of key themes are highlighted: the appropriateness of work contexts, management and supervision, interest and motivation, the ability to show one's potential as an employee, and relations with co-workers. In conclusion it is suggested that given recent findings regarding the potential benefit of person-centred mentoring for autistic adults (Ridout & Edmondson, 2017), that traditional interventions to enhance the employment prospects of autistic people should not to be driven by normative expectations, but ideally from a well-informed emancipatory ethos.

Introduction

As an autistic person, a common mantra that one hears is that people such as myself struggle with change and 'transition'. It is often assumed that simply due to one's autistic disposition[1] that one is likely to be paralysed by fear and anxiety at the notion of the smallest change of routine. To characterise all social interactions that autistic people have in such a way would be an error, yet when looked at in more depth and in context, not only individual differences between autistic people's responses are found, but also factors related to the social (dis)positionality within which autistic people live their lives.

Within this chapter, I have taken an 'aut-ethnographic' case-study approach (Milton, 2014a) to the issue of starting a new job, with particular regard as to what can be learnt from this story in the context of mentoring young autistic adults beginning a period of employment. An aut-ethnography differs from auto-ethnography in some important respects which are outlined herein. A case study can be said to involve a detailed investigation of a particular 'case' and the context within which a case exists, selected on the basis of having something of interest or revealing something of value that one can learn, from the in-depth analysis of a particular case (Creswell, 2009). Ethnography, in the broadest sense, encompasses approaches that look to describe and interpret cultural groups in everyday settings, usually through observational research with the group being studied (Creswell, 2009). As the name 'auto' suggests, auto-ethnographic research takes a self-reflective approach to build an autobiographic narrative of situated 'insider knowledge'. Similarly to ethnography, the method encourages the use of one's sociological imagination (Mills, 1959) to draw links between personal experiences and narratives and wider socially situated phenomena. In this sense, the experiences I have had regarding employment may not be 'generalisable' in any scientific sense to a wider population, but may well resonate with other autistic adults who have had to navigate various workplaces, often without any kind of support or recognition of one's needs as an employee on the autism spectrum. An auto-ethnography differs from ethnography in that it highlights the researcher's own (dis)positionality and subjectivity as an integral part of the research process.

Whilst auto-ethnographic approaches often highlight the telling of a 'coherent' story over time, I have previously argued that an 'aut-ethnography' would not necessarily be so characterised in structure (Milton, 2014a). For me, personal experiences are often fragmented and their place in terms of a sequence of time often irrelevant. Thus in this aut-ethnographic case study, I have used pertinent fragments of narrative that potentially resonate with wider social phenomena and trends.

For me, each new work experience that one has in life is an educational experience which highlights issues with transitional planning, both in terms of successes and learning from one's mistakes. It is also of importance to place one's own experiences within a wider socio-economic context when writing an ethnographic case study, as the similarities and differences in one's experiences compared to others can lead to sociological insights and practical recommendations for practice, particularly in regard to a mentoring context (explored later in this chapter).

My working life – a brief and fragmented history

My first experience of paid employment (beyond that of a paper round) came in the summer of 1996. I was 22 years old and needed to pay off some debt that I had accrued following the first year of my second attempt at an undergraduate degree. Due to my lack of experience and confidence in the job market I went for the lowest paid advert in the job centre, which at the time was in Brecon in Wales as I was staying

---

1 The term '(dis)position' is used in this chapter to refer to the dual influence of embodied neurological diversity and the socially stigmatised position in society that autistic people occupy.

with my father that summer. I was taken on at £2.12 an hour in a wool-packing factory. This involved pushing large wheeled containers of wool around a factory floor. When I left after each day I would be covered in hairs and stank of a not so pleasant odour. I struggled on by for a number of weeks until one day one of my work colleagues decided to throw a piece of dried dung across the factory floor which landed on my forehead and cut it open. I didn't go back. A number of lessons could have been learnt from this experience, but were not to be until much later in my working life. An obvious example was that such work was not the best suited to someone with extreme aversions to external sensory stimuli. Another less obvious example was the need in a workplace to make friends and allies. In this example, I did not. I remember one day saying to a co-worker that I was in the middle of doing a degree, to which they replied: 'Oh, I thought that you were thick like the rest of us'. One could make many a sociological reflection on such a comment, yet I did not manage such relations at work well and ended up with the nickname of 'Lurch' (after the character from the Addams Family), a common style of 'teasing' that I had also experienced during my school years.

Following this experience I decided to change area and stayed with my mother on the south coast of England and signed up at a temp agency supplying local factories. I worked in a number of factories that summer but primarily one producing dairy products – another not so wise choice given that I have an intolerance to dairy products. The work I acquired at this stage of my life was not at all suitable to my sensibilities, yet the overriding factor was necessity. The following year I also worked occasionally in factories and for a time as a cashier at a petrol station. None of these jobs required a formal interview at the time, something I did not excel at, having also been turned down for a job at fast-food chain restaurant.

In the autumn of the year 2000 at the age of 27 I began my first attempt at a PhD. I needed funds to pay for this course and so agreed to teach eight first-year undergraduate seminar classes for the year. At first I found the experience terrifying, and my first few classes no doubt undersold the course to the students. However I then found myself enjoying the experience. It became less stressful the more I continued to hold the seminars. Upon reflection, this was due to being able to concentrate on an area of interest to me and lead the interactions in that direction, all within tightly controlled one hour scheduled slots and thus predictable. Unfortunately this employment was to come to an end, as I was less successful in my studies and the relationship I had with my supervisor, along with running out of funds, and decided to withdraw from the course and with that the work ended. With this role, I did not know how to make the most of the opportunities that may have presented themselves to me. I lacked confidence and instead of changing supervisor early on in my PhD, I struggled on and didn't communicate my issues until relations had hit an impasse. Taking on the challenge of teaching and finding that I enjoyed leading such classes gave me a potential goal for future work however.

The following year I found out that I was to become a father. I struggled to find any work, especially that utilised qualifications in sociology, yet I managed to find work by applying to an open advert for people to work in a chain of gambling shops. In this work I did not have to impress at the interview and could manage the maths tests used to select people at training easily. However, I was less prepared for the fast-paced life of a cashier dealing with frustrated customers and lasted all of a few months in the role. The next job I took on was as a field researcher for a market research company. Again the work did not require an interview, but successful completion of a short training course. Although an interesting job for an aspiring sociologist, convincing people on the doorstep to undertake survey research was quite a task and it often took me a long time to complete a day's quota. This work was sometimes a good experience, largely in the respect of involving a largely self-sufficient way of working. Yet, being outdoors in all weathers and potentially annoying people in their homes does not lead to long-term job satisfaction, and so I managed to last nine months in this role.

My first full-time professional role came following the completion of a teacher-training course in a further education college as a lecturer in sociology and academic skills. I lasted in this role throughout my early-thirties and very much enjoyed the teaching aspects of the role. The role was not without its downsides though, including at one point collapsing in dehydration and stress and having to take a couple of weeks off work. I eventually had my position undermined via 'office politics' and was made redundant, leaving me an unemployed single-father of a then diagnosed autistic son. It was to be several months later that I was diagnosed as being on the spectrum myself. Although in this role I had learnt to make allies at work, I was less prepared for when such allies turn against you.

In recent years I have acquired work as a consultant on autism-related projects and more recently work as a researcher and in a managerial role at the National Autistic Society. In starting these roles, a simple difference to those that I started in the past was the ability to disclose as autistic. Without asking for particular 'reasonable adjustments', I have been able to show my capabilities within the field and this has helped to maintain such roles, and have colleagues that are generally more understanding of my needs as an employee. One of the most disabling aspects of being autistic is when no allowances are made at all and one is expected to fit in with non-autistic social expectations. This is inevitable pre-diagnosis and when one feels unable to disclose one's diagnosis.

Common themes

According to a large-scale conducted by the National Autistic Society (NAS, 2014), only 15% of respondents were in paid full-time employment, whilst 79% indicated that they would like such work. Although autistic people are as divergent from one another as non-autistic people are (possibly more so), it would be fair to say that some of the poor experiences of employment that I have endured are also encountered by others on the autism spectrum. Themes that emerge from my own aut-ethnographic history include: appropriateness of work, management and supervision, interest and motivation, showing potential to employers, and lastly relations with co-workers.

Appropriateness of work

Many of my poor experiences of work relate to the lack of appropriateness of work environments to my own needs as a person on the autism spectrum. From busy factory floors, to customer service, and open-plan offices, most of the work environments that I have encountered have been overloading both in amount and intensity of sensory stimuli. Work needing large amounts of undirected social interaction also increases levels of stress and exhaustion leading to potential 'burnout'. In more recent posts I have been able to carry out most of my work from home and organise my workload flexibly. This has aided my productivity immensely, yet is obviously not an option for those stuck in low-paid and highly managed work placements, as is likely to be the case for many younger people on the autism spectrum or those with learning disabilities.

Management and supervision

Before being diagnosed as being on the autism spectrum, I often had great difficulty in my relationships with those who managed me and thus had a position of power over the work that I did, often leading to poor communication, strained relations, and a lack of understanding in both directions (exemplifying the 'double empathy problem' – Milton, 2012a). Having managers that one can openly discuss one's work with without negative judgement and with full knowledge of one's diagnosis is in comparison far more preferable. Disclosure of an autism diagnosis outside a field of work related to autism may well prove more costly, as without such experience of autistic co-workers or a willingness to learn, a label can add to one's stigmatisation.

Interest and motivation

A number of autistic accounts highlight the centrality of highly-focused interests in the social 'lifeworld' of autistic people (e.g. Murray et al, 2005; Lawson, 2010; Milton, 2012b). My own personal account highlights how I have utilised my interests and strengths at various points in my employment history, sometimes to attain work in the first place, but also to maintain work where possible. Without interest and motivation, work can become little more than a tiresome chore – yet with their interests engaged people are able to take on challenges that would otherwise seem too difficult to navigate.

Showing potential

Throughout my working life, work has often not been attained nor sustained through traditional means. Being able to 'sell oneself' is not a trait often related to people on the autism spectrum, and thus being able to show one's potential through other means is often beneficial, for instance by attaining work through training courses and work placements.

Relations with co-workers

Key to longevity in a job is often the ability to work well with others. Not relating well to others and making allies at work has often led to barriers in my own career development. This is worsened however if one has to play such social 'language games' (Chown, 2014) without even the personal knowledge of one's own diagnosis. This is not to say that diagnosis will automatically lead to a full understanding of one's (dis) positionality, but it does provide a tool that can be utilised in one's interactions with potential employers.

Employment and a social model of autism

A traditional normative approach to the underemployment of autistic people would highlight the perceived deficits of autistic people, such as 'lacking a theory of mind', or 'rigidity of thought and behaviour', to suggest that it is these 'impairments' that primarily hinder autistic people from gaining and sustaining work. Also, consequently, in order to increase the numbers of autistic people in work, one would need to minimise said deficits and target problem behaviours in an attempt to 'normalise' the actions of the autistic person as much as possible. Such an approach can be seen in the guidance offered on the Autism Speaks website (Autism Speaks, 2017). This guidance includes advice such as: dressing for 'success', tips on 'grooming', how and when to give a handshake, sitting up in one's chair, facing the interviewer, using an upbeat tone of voice, and finally: smiling and making eye contact. Attempting to do all of these things when one is a passive natured, prone to stress, monotone sounding and a dyspraxic autistic person, for me simply leads to an increase in anxiety and is felt as more of a hindrance than a help. One could say that such an approach reinforces ableist and normative values that can only keep autistic people in a disadvantaged position.

When applying a social (or indeed post-social) model of autism to the issue of employment, one should not exclude the influence of embodied experience (Milton, 2014b) and the challenges that can create, yet such challenges are also seen as apparent within ever-changing and negotiated social contexts (Milton, 2013). In this respect, the themes from this aut-ethnographic case study highlight a number of important issues, from the psycho-emotional disablement (the undermining of the psycho-emotional well-being of disabled people through social oppression) of navigating normative social expectations (Milton & Moon, 2012), to the increased disempowerment that can accompany autistic people prior to their recognition as being on the autism spectrum. A person-centred approach allowing for flexibility in work environment to meet needs has led to the most successful period of my own employment history, so how does one create such a space for others in a variety of work contexts? Creating a fully 'autism-friendly' society may be an 'ideal-type model' to work toward, but it is possible when social spaces are 'owned' and led by autistic people themselves (Milton et al, 2016). Autistic-led space or 'autspace' moves far beyond the normative legal requirements of 'reasonable adjustment' and places the needs of autistic people as paramount. It is questionable to what extent such activities have affected spaces that are not autistic-led however, including autism-related events such as the Autism Show, often criticised for its lack of accessibility for autistic people themselves.

For some on the autism spectrum, the prospect of paid employment could be seen as nonsense or even exploitative. For some autistic people who also have severe learning disabilities, the concept of work or money may be alien, and thus thinking of work as a meaningful use of a person's time could be seen as exploiting their (dis)position. For more verbal autistic adults, accounts of similar issues to the ones that I have experienced in gaining and sustaining employment are plentiful. What aids one autistic person in their career development will not be the same as for the next person however, and it would be foolish to endorse some kind of 'one-size-fits-all' approach to the issue.

Future directions: befriending and mentoring

Adults on the autism spectrum who are highly verbal can have nuanced support needs that can go unrecognised within work settings. Both Access to Work and student mentoring for people on the autism spectrum are available through various schemes in the UK, yet specialist schemes are rare and research on the topic rarer still. Many of these said schemes utilise a traditional normative approach to autism (e.g. Mowat et al, 2011) critiqued by autistic activists (Milton, 2012b). The only area of mentoring for people on the autism spectrum to have begun to gain the attention of researchers has been student mentoring schemes for college and university students. This gap in the research literature led to a two-year pilot study being funded to establish a mentoring scheme for adults on the spectrum aged 18+, based at London South Bank University and designed with input from people on the autism spectrum and their families and supporters. Its effectiveness was evaluated using both quantitative and qualitative methods. The project was framed within an 'emancipatory research' context and guided by personal construct theory (PCT). Whilst the project was only a pilot study that matched twelve mentors with mentees, some of the mentees who participated were young people starting work or on apprenticeships or vocational courses.

PCT was a psychotherapeutic theory developed by George Kelly in the 1950's. Kelly was critical of the dominant psychology theories of the time – psychoanalysis and behaviourism – and felt that they were inadequate for helping people in a counselling or therapeutic setting. Kelly was more concerned with what he called the 'jackass in the middle', the conscious subject and their personal constructions of social reality. In order to increase feelings of well-being, this theory posited that one has to start with how an individual constructs their viewpoint rather than imposing one upon them. Thus, the influence of PCT on the mentoring project is due to the person-centred nature of this theoretical approach and its long standing use within mentoring and counselling services. This framework, along with a wider framing of the project within a social model of autism/disability, led to a training day being devised for mentors that not only covers these issues, but also looks at dominant psychological theories in the field from a critical standpoint, describing them as potentially flawed tools rather than factual (Milton et al, 2017). The findings from this project has shown a strong indication that the well-being and employment prospects of autistic people can be significantly improved by such a program of support (Ridout & Edmondson, 2017), and makes a significant shift in approach regarding the 'desired outcomes' of such autistic learners, from a normative to an emancipator paradigm.

References

Autism Speaks (2015). Available at: www.autismspeaks.org (accessed September 2017).

Chown N (2014) More on the ontological status of autism and double empathy. *Disability and Society* **29** (10) 1672–1676.

Creswell J (2009) *Research Design: Qualitative, quantitative, and mixed methods approaches* (3rd edition). London: SAGE Publications Ltd.

Lawson W (2010) *The Passionate Mind: How people with autism learn*. London: Jessica Kingsley.

Mills CW (1959) *The Sociological Imagination*. Oxford: Oxford University Press.

Milton D (2012a) On the ontological status of autism: the 'double empathy problem'. *Disability and Society* **27** (6) 883–887.

Milton D (2012b) *So What Exactly is Autism?* Autism Education Trust.

Milton D (2013) "Filling in the gaps", a micro-sociological analysis of autism [online]. *Autonomy: the Journal of Critical Interdisciplinary Autism Studies* **1** (2). Available at: http://www.larry-arnold.net/Autonomy/index.php/autonomy/article/view/7/html (accessed September 2017).

Milton D (2014a) Becoming autistic: an aut-ethnography. Cutting edge psychiatry in practice. *Autism Spectrum Disorder* **4** 185–192.

Milton D (2014b) Embodied sociality and the conditioned relativism of dispositional diversity. *Autonomy: the Journal of Critical Interdisciplinary Autism Studies*. Vol. 1(3). Available at: http://www.larry-arnold.net/Autonomy/index.php/autonomy/article/view/32/html (accessed September 2017).

Milton D, Martin M & Melham P (2016) Beyond reasonable adjustment: autistic-friendly spaces and Universal Design. In: D Milton and N Martin (Eds) *Autism and Intellectual Disabilities in Adults, Volume 1* (pp81–86) Hove: Pavilion Publishing & Media Ltd.

Milton D & Moon L (2012) The normalisation agenda and the psycho-emotional disablement of autistic people. *Autonomy: the Journal of Critical Interdisciplinary Autism Studies* **1** (1). Available at: from: http://www.larry-arnold.net/Autonomy/index.php/autonomy/article/view/9 (accessed September 2017).

Milton D, Sims T, Dawkins G, Martin N & Mills R (2017) The development and evaluation of a mentor training programme for those working with autistic adults. *Good Autism Practice* **18** (1) 25–33.

Mowat C, Cooper A & Gilson L (2011) *Supporting Students on the Autism Spectrum: Student mentor guidelines*. National Autistic Society: London.

Murray D, Lesser M & Lawson W (2005) Attention, monotropism and the diagnostic criteria for autism. *Autism* **9** (2) 136–156.

NAS Ask autism (2015) *Employment and Autism conference*.

National Autistic Society (2014) *Employment Services* [online]. Available at: http://www.autism.org.uk/working-with/employment-services.aspx (accessed September 2017).

Ridout S & Edmondson M (2017) Cygnet Mentoring Project: combined experiences from a mentor and a mentee [online]. *Autonomy: the Critical Journal of Interdisciplinary Autism Studies* **1** (5). Available at: http://www.larry-arnold.net/Autonomy/index.php/autonomy/article/view/AR20/html (accessed September 2017).

Mental health and autism

Dr Eddie Chaplin

Abstract

Good mental health is characterised by emotional, psychological, and social well-being. Although autism is not a mental health problem, it has historically been associated with some mental illness, such as schizophrenia. The number of autistic people with mental health problems is difficult to estimate and establishing a mental health diagnosis can be problematic because of overlap of symptoms. However it is important to note that autistic people can experience the full range of mental health problems from severe mental illness, such as psychotic or bipolar disorders, to common mental health problems such as mild depression and anxiety. This chapter offers an overview of some of the more common mental health problems and strategies to support autistic people to access mental health care.

Introduction

When we have poor mental health, it can affect our everyday lives. We may feel stressed or react poorly to stressful events that we could have coped with previously, our behaviour can change and we may lose interest in everyday things we would normally enjoy, or neglect ourselves or others around us. It could be argued that autistic people face more threats to their mental well-being because of societal barriers that can affect and limit opportunities, inclusion and access to services that others take for granted. This can often create increased distress and anxiety for autistic people. Distress and poor mental health can manifest in different ways, e.g. a person may be eating or sleeping too much or too little, feeling anxious or depressed, feeling worthless, being forgetful and unable to concentrate, being angry, experiencing changes in mood and ruminating over events. For some these symptoms may worsen and a person can become mentally ill. Signs of more serious mental illness can include hallucinations and delusions, thoughts of self-harm or suicide, and the person losing touch with reality. There is no one singular cause of mental illness but best guess is that it is a combination of biological, psychological, social and environmental factors.

Autism and mental health

Although autism is not a mental health problem, originally the term was used by Bleuler to describe symptoms of schizophrenia (Bleuler, 1950). In 1943, Kanner published *Autistic Disturbances of Affective Contact* which described autism as a separate disorder. Studying a group of eight boys and three girls Kanner reported a unique syndrome that previously would have been labelled as schizophrenic or feeble minded. Although autism is not a mental illness there are links between autism and certain mental health conditions such as schizophrenia, mood disorders and ADHD in terms of possible shared generic aetiology and symptoms (Burback & der Zwaag, 2009).

Prevalence studies to the extent of mental health problems in autistic people can be difficult to conduct, for a number of reasons. Many studies have used small sample sizes or been conducted in locations with higher levels of psychiatric morbidity such as hospitals. Establishing a diagnosis of autism when someone has mental health problems can be difficult; there are issues with differentiating symptoms associated with autism that may also be present in serious mental illness such as schizophrenia, for instance concrete thinking, echolalia and so on. Even when it is known a person has autism, diagnosing mental illness can also be difficult. Although there is an overlap of symptoms with autism and a number of mental health or developmental conditions, the presentation and onset of these are often different. For example, in schizophrenia fantasy may be mistaken for delusions, preferring one's own company and seemingly appearing uninterested could be mistaken for negative symptoms. Some autistic people with mental illness may also experience an increase in autistic-related behaviour which can conceal mental health concerns and make identification difficult.

Autistic people can experience the full range of mental health problems from severe mental illness, such as psychotic or bipolar disorders, to common mental health problems such as mild depression and anxiety. Mental health assessment for autistic people should consider the individuals needs and abilities. Whatever the support needs are of individuals it is also useful to obtain collateral information (assuming consent) to verify information and in some cases to give information if the individual has difficulties articulating or recognising their problem.

There are a number of common mental health and neurodevelopmental diagnoses that may co-exist with autism which are described below.

Neurodevelopmental conditions

ADHD

It is estimated that between 37-85% of children with autism have symptoms of ADHD, and when they do occur they lead to increased morbidity (Leitner, 2014). ADHD can be misdiagnosed as bipolar or personality disorder and ADHD and autism co-occurs at high levels (McCarthy et al, 2016). However, given how this may complicate presentation, ADHD can be often missed, meaning the person is unable to access appropriate treatment. This will impact on the person both now and in the future. With ADHD and autism there are a number of symptoms common to both conditions such as impulsivity, irritability, inattention and hyperactivity. Although symptoms may be similar, the responses of autistic people to various interventions may differ from those of people without autism. For example, ADHD is often treated by stimulant medication with good effect in terms of reduction of symptoms, however, autistic characteristics will not be altered by such medication. Medication will not work to make social learning or behaviour more neurotypical, for example in an autistic person. (Any medical interventions related to ADHD will be of little use on their own and should always be delivered within a social framework, with support offered to unpick behaviours and address any challenges that threaten quality of life or social exclusion. Without this any progress made with medication for ADHD may not be sustained.)

Intellectual disability

It is estimated that 50-70% of autistic people have an intellectual disability (Matson & Shoemaker, 2009). The accuracy of this estimate is open to question given the increased awareness and diagnostic improvements which have contributed to the broadening criteria of autism over time. By definition people with intellectual disability will have issues with social interaction, memory, recall and understanding of complex information. The degree to which this occurs is different from individual to individual. Intellectual impairment is usually present from birth but may be acquired as a result of an accident or severe illness such as meningitis.

Individuals with intellectual disabilities have higher rates of mental health problems than the general population (Cooper et al, 2007). However there is no firm agreement relating to individuals with intellectual disability and autism. A study in Canada reported that adults with intellectual disabilities and autism were less likely to have psychosis when compared to individuals without autism (Lunsky et al, 2009). Whereas, Bradley et al (2004) reported adolescents with autism and severe intellectual disabilities were likely to experience increased episodes of mental health problems compared to those without autism. Tsakanikos et al (2006) found a similar prevalence of mental health problems in individuals with intellectual disabilities and autism. Given the wide variation in mental health problems more research is required for greater understanding.

Psychotic conditions

Schizophrenia

When the term infantile autism was first used there was an erroneous and unhelpful association with childhood schizophrenia, which has since been discredited. Now it is understood that secondary mental health concerns can occur alongside autism. Estimates vary as to the prevalence of schizophrenia in autism from of 0-6% (Skokauskas & Gallagher, 2010). Although these conditions do coexist they can also be confused and mistaken for each other. For example, a person with autism may hold fixed beliefs that may appear odd and this can be difficult for people who do not understand autism to distinguish from delusions. Hallucinations may be difficult to recognise correctly particularly in those who are less able to express themselves verbally. It is thought persecutory ideas might be linked to problems in attention or explained not as a psychotic symptom, but as a consequence of Theory of Mind or the individuals' experiences of social alienation and exclusion, which may or may not be linked to reality. Where there is doubt that a person has a diagnosis of schizophrenia or autism, considerations include whether there were features of autism during childhood, and the nature and extent of what is being considered as psychotic symptoms. For example, many autistic people may adopt alternative or imaginary worlds as a coping strategy which may have stemmed from childhood. The stories can be very convincing to someone who does not know the person, to the point of them being mistaken as delusional thought.

Mood and anxiety conditions

Depression

Autistic people across the spectrum can have difficulty describing their emotions and feelings. Those who are more able to communicate verbally are more likely to report depressive symptoms (Sterling et al, 2008). In depression the most common symptoms, as well as low mood, can include loss of interest in pleasurable activities, reduced functioning, disturbed sleep and appetite, and a slowing-down of thought and a reduction of physical movements in an individual, where in severe cases they may result in stupor. All of which assist the diagnosis of depression, with a recent onset of or increase in maladaptive behaviour such as self-injury or aggression, and/or a decrease in adaptive behaviour, such as reduced self-care or worsening of stereotyped or ritualistic behaviour, such as echolalia, may indicate the presence of a depressive disorder. However, autistic people may have problems identifying their own symptoms of depression for a number of reasons including:

→ Alexithymia, where people are unable to recognise feelings and emotions.

→ Being unable to express or articulate their experience. The person may not link experiences together such as not eating or sleeping, or feeling down. They may be poor reporters or unable to put together a chronology of events.

→ Being unable to understand their experience in the context of abstract concepts such as poor mental health.

Compared to others, autistic people may struggle to express their feelings. It is therefore important when supporting someone's mental well-being that they are offered strategies to engage, understand and, where possible, manage their own mental health. Some ways of doing this include:

→ Keeping a diary.

→ Use of self-reporting measures which are adapted to suit the person's preferred way of communicating e.g. written, use of symbols denoting happiness or sadness.

→ Being able to talk to someone.

→ Use of a health passport and listing things that the individual enjoys and makes them happy.

→ To know what to do and how to get help.

All of these strategies are adapted form self-help guides used in the general population and as such the treatment autistic people will receive for mood disorders such as cognitive behavioural therapy (CBT) will not differ, although there may be adaptations to the process to ensure equity for the person to engage with the process (Spain *et al*, 2015). Medications to treat depression are the same although they have not been tested on adults with ASD who may be at increased risk of side effects or adverse reactions.

Bipolar affective disorder

Bipolar disorder is characterised by episodes of 'highs and 'lows' of mood called mania or hypomania and depression. There are two types of bipolar affective disorder; type 1, which involves episodes of mania and depression and type 2, where mood is still elevated with milder episodes of hypomania, which alternate with periods of severe depression. When a person is manic or hypomanic they may present as being irritable, having increased energy and decreased need for sleep, decreased appetite, being reckless, making poor choices and having pressure of speech, grandiose delusions and high-risk behaviours which are out of character for the person when they are well. These can include overspending, or reckless driving, for example.

Anxiety

Anxiety covers a range of conditions, which include generalised anxiety disorders, social anxiety phobias and panic disorders. All of us at some stage will experience occasional and mild anxiety. Anxiety becomes a problem when it becomes more severe and where the person becomes irrational or unable to cope in everyday situations. Examples may include where the person may misinterpret physical symptoms of anxiety such as hyperventilating, rapid pulse and breathing or stomach upset as something more sinister which makes the person more anxious. Although these are feelings that many people will have experienced, for anxiety to be diagnosed symptoms need to be present for more than two weeks. Data is not reliable on the extent to which anti-anxiety medication is in use in the general population, but good practice indicates it should only be used short term for severe anxiety. Psychological interventions are commonly used to treat anxiety including such techniques as deep breathing particularly for mild anxiety. Treatment is focused according to how the person presents, and could include challenging negative or 'incorrect' thoughts and assumptions, for example a person feels their heart is racing so they hyperventilate and as a result feel dizzy. Anxiety about underlying medical reasons for a racing heart may need to be addressed. The individual may feel that they are having a heart attack and are going to die. Having ruled out any physical cause the treatment would involve looking at the symptoms in the context of anxiety and thinking about ways in which with practice they could be managed effectively by the individual. Treatment may also use role play for strategies to manage difficult situations. In the case of phobias the use of graded exposure to the feared situation may be helpful. Medication should only be considered in short spells for acute, severe anxiety but not as an ongoing treatment.

It can be highly dangerous to make assumptions based on erroneous evaluation of what is causing the anxiety. Below is an extract from an article written by an autistic person.

> *'In this regard I remember a situation from my own childhood at the end of my time at the kindergarten when I broke a thigh falling from a climbing scaffold. I cried and screamed all the way in the ambulance to the clinic but not because I was in pain. On the contrary, I was and still am today rather insensitive to pain. But already on the way in the ambulance they cut my trousers I was wearing and those were my favourite trousers. I could hardly calm myself and therefore of course the pain killers they hurriedly gave me did not help against my sorrows. When my mother saw me at the hospital she knew immediately what the problem was and she then managed to calm me down after a while.'*
> (Preissmann, 2017, p118)

This illustrates the need for communication and not always assuming you know what is best and what has caused the anxiety.

Although it is thought that autistic people experience higher rates of obsessive compulsive disorder (OCD), a number may also misdiagnosed with the condition because repetitive behaviours (which are a core symptom of autism) can be misinterpreted as OCD. One way to test this is the level of distress experienced by the person. An autistic individual will not necessarily be distressed by their repetitive behaviours which will often serve a positive function as a way to reduce stress. Whereas if the behaviour is as a result of OCD, there will be notable anxiety and the function of the behaviour will differ. For example, the person might feel compelled to repeatedly wash their hands for fear of germs, or recheck they have turned off the gas for fear of explosions or continually checking locks for fear of intruders.

Mental health assessment of autism and mental health problems

The experiences of autistic people and being autistic in the social world that we live in may increase the risk of mental health problems. These include:

- → communication
- → life events
- → loneliness and isolation
- → low self-esteem
- → being unable to articulate symptoms or recognise or describe emotions
- → interpreting questions literally
- → struggling to recall events chronologically
- → poor memory and concentration
- → poor quality of life
- → poverty of experience in terms of work, leisure, relationships
- → lack of ability to recognise basic emotions.

As autism is a spectrum condition, and everyone is an individual, the above examples will not relate to every autistic person, as general predictors of mental health and presentation will differ person-to-person in all individuals with mental health problems. Once autism is suspected, the mental state examination should take into account the key typical indicators of autism i.e. social communication, interaction and what are commonly referred to as restrictive interests. This terminology can be confusing as restrictive interests may be source of enjoyment and will not necessarily restrict the person. In fact, narrow in-depth interests can often afford opportunities to improve social networks, and inclusion with others who share similar passions.

Autistic people might struggle to describe their mental state or recall symptoms as they may not associate them with what is being asked by a health professional. Changes in behaviour may alert those around the person to deteriorating mental health, such as whether the person becomes increasingly aloof or distant or begins to communicate differently from the way that is typical for them; for example becoming more or less talkative. Other signs can include speech which may be less expressive or more monotonous than is usual for the individual. Some autistic people are much more articulate than others, but the content of conversation may well focus on the person's in-depth interests. If this is usual for them it is not a cause for concern but significant changes in typical communication style merits monitoring in the first instance. Non-verbal cues may be difficult for other people to interpret,

Figure 1: Supporting someone to seek help for their mental health. Adapted from Chaplin *et al* (2016).

Adaptation	Rationale
Longer appointment times.	To aid improved communication and comprehension.
Appointment times at the beginning or end of the day.	To avoid long waiting times or busy waiting rooms, which can increase anxiety.
Accessible information. Consider using pictures or symbols to augment verbal communication.	To aid comprehension.
Preparedness – person with autism and staff supporting them. Understand what the appointment is for, bring all relevant information and any communication aids or accessible information that could assist the consultation.	To improve the quality of consultation and enable a comprehensive exchange of information to inform diagnosis, care and treatment.
Talking directly to the individual with autism and only later clarifying with carers or family.	To value and involve the person with autism and provide person-centred care.
Anchoring events i.e. take your medicine after the late night news or 'remember when we did X...' rather than saying '4 weeks ago...'	To enable improved communication.
Environment – free from background noise, flickering lights, and medical equipment that is not required.	To reduce anxiety and improve receptive communication. Autistic people may get distressed if overloaded with sensory stimuli.
Check that the person has understood what you have said by asking them to explain it back to you.	To check comprehension and avoid acquiescence.
If using complex or technical words, check that you both have the same understanding of what is meant by that word. Conversely avoid jargon, idiom and metaphor as these may be taken literally e.g. 'hop on the bed and let me examine you'.	To avoid misdiagnosis or diagnostic overshadowing and facilitate communication.
Make the environment as friendly and predictable as possible or complete the assessment at a venue that the person feels most comfortable in. This may include attention to sensory stimuli such as noise, lighting, temperature etc.	To reduce anxiety and increase rapport. Autistic people may experience sensory hyper or hypo sensitivity that may cause distress.
Ask the same questions in different ways at different times during the appointment.	To check comprehension and avoid acquiescence, particularly in those with intellectual disabilities.
Ensure that you fully understand what the concerns or difficulties are and that you fully understand what is normal for the person with autism. Act on any changes that are reported and consider possible physical or mental health diagnoses.	To avoid diagnostic overshadowing and ensure timely access to appropriate healthcare.
Conduct a thorough assessment of mental and physical health, which could include: → physical examination and appropriate investigations → medication history (neuroleptics, anti-hypertensives, steroids etc.) → adverse effects of drugs (including anti-depressants) → assessment to exclude other differential diagnoses. Risk assessment (for both self-harm, self-neglect, harm to others and adult safeguarding) is important.	Differential diagnosis and diagnostic overshadowing. Sometimes autistic people can experience different or 'atypical' signs and symptoms of illnesses or they seek help at a late stage of an illness which makes it appear different to how it might usually present. This can mean that serious illness is not diagnosed or incorrectly diagnosed leading to delays in treatment.

for example the autistic person may have an unusual, fixed or exaggerated facial expression. Knowing the autistic person is important in order to ascertain whether there is any change. Frequently autistic people experience sensory issues such as sensitivity to light or noise and mannerisms that offer comfort such as rocking or twirling fingers are not unusual. It is always important to intervene with understanding. Rocking for example may well be a functional calming behaviour for which no intervention is necessary.

When assessing mental health there are a number of things that are taken into consideration, e.g. has their mood changed, what are the current behaviours that can be observed, are these new or have they always been part of the person's normal pattern and range of behaviours? Other information that might help includes whether the person has been in contact with school or intellectual services or whether there is a history of autism or other neurodevelopmental conditions in the family, particularly among first (e.g. parents or siblings) or second degree (e.g. grandparents, aunts and uncles) relatives. Physical health can also be a factor, for example the presence of epilepsy which is seen at higher rates in autistic people. When taking a developmental history, it is also worth including social aspects such as behaviour and interaction with others, as well as milestones and other developmental markers.

Supporting someone who is receiving care and treatment

When supporting an individual to look after their mental health or to seek help from mental health services, you will need to provide emotional, psychological and practical support. This might be encouraging the person to lead a healthy lifestyle and to use coping strategies such as relaxation techniques. Where there is a need to seek help, a person can be supported to prepare for appointments by having all necessary information available ahead of time, such as a list of current medications, history of current problems and support plans. For the person to get an equitable standard of healthcare you might need to ask that reasonable adjustment is made (see Figure 1). This might mean requesting longer appointment times or information in an accessible format for the individual. This is to ensure that communication is appropriate to the individual and that they have been given sufficient time to understand and reply to questions. Following the appointment, the person may be asked to do tasks to monitor their health such as recording and monitoring particular behaviours such as sleeping and eating or feelings of anxiety or feeling low in mood.

Conclusion

Mental health is important to our quality of life and our everyday functioning. Everyone will experience threats to their mental well-being and for some this can develop into more serious mental health problems which will mean people need to seek access to mental health services. Even those who do seek formal help will often rely on their own coping strategies for dealing with adversity or make use of health promotions such as adopting a healthy lifestyle. Autistic people present with the same mental health problems as in the general population, but these may be more difficult to detect in autistic people whose symptoms may present atypically. The core features of autism may mask symptoms so assessment should be modified to take this into account.

References

Bleuler E (1950) *Dementia Praecox or the Group of Schizophrenias* (original 1911, translated 1950 by J. Zinkin. New York: International Universities Press.

Bradley EA, Summers JA, Wood H & Bryson SE (2004) Comparing rates of psychiatric and behavior disorders in adolescents and young adults with severe intellectual disability with and without autism. *Journal of Autism and Developmental Disorders* **34** (2) 151–161.

Burbach JPH & van der Zwaag B (2009) Contact in the genetics of autism and schizophrenia. *Trends in Neurosciences* **32** (2) 69–72.

Chaplin E, Marshall-Tate K & Hardy S (2016) *An Introduction to Supporting the Mental Health of People with Intellectual Disabilities: A guide for professionals, support staff and families.* Brighton: Pavilion Publishing & Media.

Cooper SA, Smiley E, Morrison J, Williamson A & Allan L (2007) Mental ill-health in adults with intellectual disabilities: prevalence and associated factors. *The British Journal of Psychiatry* **190** (1) 27–35.

Kanner L (1943) Autistic disturbances of affective contact. *Nervous Child* **2** (3) 217–250.

Leitner Y (2014) The co-occurrence of autism and attention deficit hyperactivity disorder in children – what do we know? *Frontiers in Human Neuroscience* **29** (8) 268.

Lunsky Y, Gracey C & Bradley E (2009) Adults with autism spectrum disorders using psychiatric hospitals in Ontario: clinical profile and service needs. *Research in Autism Spectrum Disorders* **3** (4) 1006–1013.

Matson JL & Shoemaker M (2009) Intellectual disability and its relationship to autism spectrum disorders. *Research in Developmental Disabilities* **30** (6) 1107–1114.

McCarthy J, Chaplin E, Underwood L, Forrester A, Hayward H, Sabet J, Young S, Asherson P, Mills R & Murphy D (2016) Characteristics of prisoners with neurodevelopmental disorders and difficulties. *Journal of Intellectual Disability Research* **60** (3) 201–206.

Preissmann C (2017) Autism and healthcare. *Advances in Autism* **3** (3) 115–124.

Skokauskas N & Gallagher L (2012) Mental health aspects of autistic spectrum disorders in children. *Journal of Intellectual Disability Research* **56** (3) 248–257.

Spain D, Sin J, Chalder T, Murphy D & Happe F (2015) Cognitive behaviour therapy for adults with autism spectrum disorders and psychiatric co-morbidity: a review. *Research in Autism Spectrum Disorders* **9** 151–162.

Sterling L, Dawson G, Estes A & Greenson J (2008) Characteristics associated with presence of depressive symptoms in adults with autism spectrum disorder. *Journal of Autism and Developmental Disorders* **38** (6) 1011–1018.

Tsakanikos E, Sturmey P, Costello H, Holt G & Bouras N (2007) Referral trends in mental health services for adults with intellectual disability and autism spectrum disorders. *Autism* **11** (1) 9–17.

Autism, learning disability, and the criminal justice system

Dr Luke Beardon and Dr Libby Gaskell

Abstract

This chapter explores some of the issues that might relate to autistic individuals who come into contact with the criminal justice system (CJS). With an underlying theme suggesting that being autistic may put the individual at a disadvantage in this area, the authors outline some of the key areas as they understand them that should be taken into account when understanding the 'autistic experience'. The chapter deliberately identifies autism in the first instance with a narrative around autism and the CJS with subsequent text identifying concepts relating to autism with additional co-morbid learning disabilities. Finally, the authors identify some key points that might help improve practice and decrease risk to the autistic population.

Introduction

Being autistic does not preclude one from being criminal – in the legal sense, and in the moral sense. In other words, being autistic is never an excuse for deliberately and knowingly breaking the law. However, we[1] believe that there may be compelling arguments within the autism field to suggest that *some* autistic[2] individuals will break the law but will do so without intent, nor with a full understanding that they are behaving in a manner that might be deemed unlawful. In such cases, we conclude that within the criminal justice system (CJS) as a whole, unless a person's autism is well understood and reasonable adjustments are made, then individuals might be being discriminated against under the Equality Act (2010). If, as we suggest, there are components in some individual cases of autism that lead to specific behaviours that lead to law breaking – and autism is subsequently not taken into account in terms of understanding the correlation (or otherwise) between the *mens rea* (the intention or knowledge) and *actus reus* (objective element of the crime) – then we are unconvinced that the legal system is fairly treating such autistic individuals.

In order to frame our argument we are basing our presentation of autism by building on Beardon's Theory of Disadvantage (2017) in which he suggests that autism can be understood in terms of disadvantage (as opposed to a medical-deficit-based model often seen within diagnostic criteria such as the DSM–5). Beardon's perspective is that being autistic in a world dominated by non–autistic populations, which we refer to as the predominant neurotype (PNT) (Beardon, 2008), often puts the autistic person at a disadvantage. We believe this to be the case in many ways within the CJS. Essentially, Beardon's equation of autism + environment = outcome is one we subscribe to in the context of the CJS – and we will now outline some of the areas in which it is possible that being autistic might lead to being disadvantaged.

This narrative is based on doctoral research, experiences with expert witness cases, as well as personal narratives from individuals who have been arrested. Not all points raised will be relevant in all cases; autistic people as individuals need to be treated as such. However, we do raise issues that we believe are worthy of consideration when engaging with autistic people who are in contact with the CJS.

We deliberately do not delve into the technicalities of the CJS, instead we have provided a list of additional reading material that readers can pursue should they wish to do so. Please do contact us for any clarification or follow up required.

Point of arrest

Obviously being arrested can be stressful for anyone. However, stress can be dealt with in several different ways, and many autistic people are in a heightened state of anxiety much of the time as a base state, so it can be concluded that during an arrest the additional stress may mean that they are at point of autistic meltdown. This may well lead to additional problems for the arresting officers, in particular if the individual is apparently (or actually) resisting arrest. It may be that there is little that can be done about this if the arresting officer is making the arrest without any foreknowledge. If, however, the individual can clearly identify themselves as autistic then it might be worth considering how an arrest might be made in order not to exacerbate a situation which will disadvantage the autistic person. For example, many autistic individuals at times of extreme stress will 'shut down' – effectively being unable to communicate or understand what is happening. Some might need extra time to process information. It is all too easy to understand how a difficult situation for an autistic individual could become vastly worse if the individual's presentation is not understood. Some individuals may simply require time to reduce their own anxiety without being overloaded with attempted communication or physical contact, so if at all possible allow the individual time and space to do so.

---
1 'we' refers to the authors
2 We use 'autistic' rather than 'person with autism' to reflect the majority view of autistic adults as noted in Kenny *et al* (2016)

Sensory issues

As is becoming increasingly acknowledged autistic individuals will have differing sensory profiles in comparison to the PNT. Some ways in which this might disadvantage an individual within the CJS include:

→ **Being handcuffed**

For someone who is tactile sensitive, being handcuffed may manifest itself as pain – in some cases this could potentially be extreme. There are several self-reported examples of extreme hypersensitivity to touch, so it is worth noting that if there is an alternative to being handcuffed, it should be considered.

→ **Being forced into a spit hood (hoods to prevent spitting or biting)**

Being in a situation where one finds it difficult to see, along with the feeling of being confined, could be extremely stressful for some autistic individuals, and should be avoided whenever possible.

→ **Being in close proximity to others**

Some individuals find close proximity, including touch, extremely invasive. If this is the case then giving the person some space might be enough to alleviate risk of extreme distress. Skin on skin contact may also be painful, so reducing or eliminating this might help.

→ **Being overloaded by sensory information**

This covers a whole range of potential issues within the sensory domain. An individual could become overwhelmed (and thus disadvantaged) by lighting, sounds, smells, touch, changes in temperature – almost anything. Within a cell environment it might be possible to make necessary adjustments in order to reduce risk of disadvantage; similarly, any interview room or area an autistic person is exposed to should be considered for its sensory impact.

→ **Being restrained**

This is in a similar vein to the sensory information outlined above, but warrants its own specified point. There are many autobiographical accounts that identify touch as being highly problematic, so physical restraint should be viewed in a cautionary manner.

It is worth noting that extremes in sensory sensitivity are highly likely to be exacerbated by factors such as heightened anxiety – so in more anxious situations a person's sensory sensitivities are likely to cause more issues than when in a calm state.

Communication

Communication issues have been identified within the autistic population ever since the first definitions of autism arose. While general understanding of what those communication issues might be have developed, there is still a lack of understanding within society as to how communication might impact on an autistic person. It is entirely possible that within the CJS assumptions about a person's communication will be made, based on the level of expressive verbal ability that is being used. For instance, if an individual's expressive language is of a high standard, it might be assumed that their level of comprehension is equally as accurate – and this might not be the case for the autistic individual. In contrast, not having a voice (e.g. some people may be unable to express themselves verbally) might not mean that the person lacks understanding. As is so often the case, each person will need to have their own communication needs understood before any reasonable adjustments are made. Some people may prefer to use written forms of communication rather than verbal, for example.

For some, differences in communication styles might be the reason why law breaking was an issue in the first instance. Having absolute faith that what someone is saying is inevitably the 'truth', for example (which is a characteristic that some autistic individuals will have) might mean that a person is extremely vulnerable to coercion. Believing what a person says without question – for example a person's age (in relation to consensual sex) – can be a huge issue. If a person were to simply believe a sexual partner when age is discussed – despite seemingly obvious contradictions (e.g. in looks or circumstance) – then he or she could inadvertently be breaking statutory rape laws. It may well be that any prosecution would subsequently find it difficult to believe that anyone would unquestioningly believe a person, taking them 'at face value'.

Nonverbal communication might also increase disadvantage. Not reading facial gestures in the manner they are intended (along with other nonverbal communications such as prosody, or body language) can cause misunderstanding and conflict.

Social naivety

Autism is often regarded as being linked closely to issues with socialising. This is not to suggest that we are inferring that the autistic person is a problem; more that the way autistic people socialise may differ from the PNT and this may cause clashes and increase risk of disadvantage to the autistic person.

What might be social 'norms' for the PNT might not apply for the autistic person. One of the most obvious examples of this that has led to recorded accounts of arrests for stalking type behaviour and/or harassment is how one (autistic) person might mis-read social signals leading them to believe that another person is interested in them as a friend or as a potential romantic partner. If this is the case then the autistic person might become increasingly anxious at the lack of reciprocity in terms of responding to requests for interaction (e.g. not replying to emails, not answering the phone) to the point of behaving in ways that are considered criminal.

Difficulty in seeing the bigger picture, cause and effect

While central coherence (i.e. a limited ability to understand context or 'see the bigger picture') has long been debated within autism theory it is clear that some autistic people do find that their focus (and understanding) might be limited to isolated detail rather than processing the bigger picture. In such cases it might be the case that an individual could break the law without understanding that they are doing so. For example, keeping goods in one's house is not a crime, harbouring stolen goods, on the other hand, is. For the person who does not naturally identify the link between goods being stolen, and keeping goods at a home address, this is clearly a problem.

Problematic cross–neurological theory of mind

Many autistic people have problems with understanding the perspectives, views, emotional states, and behaviours of others who do not share their neurotype – what Beardon refers to as difficulties in 'cross-neurological theory of mind' and Milton (2012) as 'the double empathy problem'. In relation to risk of law breaking, this may come into play in a number of ways. For example, deception is something that is linked closely with theory of mind, so it might be that an autistic person can be deceived easily into breaking the law. Some individuals will simply take statements to be true without question, even though it might be readily apparent to others that statements are clearly not altogether accurate. It might be very difficult for practitioners within the CJS to accept that those within their custody genuinely do find it difficult to understand what others might take for granted.

Many autistic individuals will find that they either do not understand the intent of others or they do not even question it. This can lead to higher risks of coercion, as well as increased vulnerability to being abused in various ways (which might lead to the person being a victim or an unknowing perpetrator). For example, being told that they should behave in a certain manner (or engage in a certain activity) and in return they will be rewarded (and for some, the reward might be as simple as the promise of friendship) might be enough for the person to do so without question of intent.

Being assessed by a jury of 'peers' and general presentation to others

Autism is known as an 'invisible disability' – in other words there isn't anything in terms of presentation that is shared by all autistic people, so it's not possible to 'see' autism (which is neurological in origin). However, being autistic can have an impact on how someone presents themselves. In some cases, this might disadvantage a person. For example lack of eye contact, which is a commonality within the autistic population, might incorrectly be taken as a sign of suspicion. In a similar vein, some autistic individuals either won't display emotional expression on their faces, or their facial expression might not reflect their emotional state. Either of these might bias others; a jury, for example. It is interesting to note that the CJS claims to use a jury of peers – we raise the question of whether a group of (presumably) non-autistic jurors would rightly be considered a jury of peers for an autistic defendant?

Autistic logic

We believe that a potentially useful way of understanding autistic behaviour is to explore the concept of autistic logic. For example, problems with cross-neurological theory of mind might lead to an autistic logic of thinking 'Well, *I* know for a fact I am not intending any harm in my behaviour so therefore logically I am not doing anything wrong'. In a similar vein to the previous 'stalking' example, if the individual knows full well in their own head that they intend no harm they may logically believe that they are not breaking any laws.

Most people, it would be fair enough to assume, don't know all the laws of the land – and yet most people would probably be able to have a reasonable understanding of what might constitute law breaking. We suggest that this might not be the case for the autistic person who is basing their reasoning on their own logic, as this might differ considerably from the legal framework in which they find themselves. This in turn would place the person at a huge disadvantage, both in terms of inadvertently breaking the law, and subsequent risks of prosecution. For example, a person may be advised to plead guilty in return for a caution – but if the person refuses to do so believing that they have done nothing wrong they might end up being prosecuted.

Autism and a learning disability

Autism and the concept of a learning disability are two separate entities in that they are two very different things, and can exist independently of each other. That said, some people with autism might have a degree of learning disability, which could add to the disadvantages they may encounter within the CJS that have been outlined. A learning disability can be defined as a significant impairment in intellectual, adaptive, and social functioning that is present before adulthood, where assistance is needed with social reasoning and problem solving (British Psychological Society, 2000). The following discussion applies to those with a learning disability, but may also apply to those with autism if they were to have a learning disability. Similarly to the previous discussion, these components are suggested difficulties that may be encountered by people with learning disabilities in the CJS, but they may not be true of all those with learning disabilities.

The offending behaviour

As is suggestive in the definition above, people with a learning disability are likely to have limitations in cognitive problem solving skills and/or an ability to engage in enhanced consequential thinking. As such, it is likely that in some cases, offending behaviour may not have been fuelled by criminal intent but by difficulties to fully comprehend and fully understand the penalties of unlawful actions.

In addition, it is important to consider this population systemically, in order to understand their experiences of their social worlds. From first-hand accounts, people with learning disabilities who engaged in offending behaviour have discussed their lack of social support, be that from family, professionals, or through a lack of friendships. This social isolation can mean people with learning disabilities are vulnerable to exploitation and coercion into acting in a criminal way by more able peers, where the person with a learning disability mistakes exploitation for friendship. Gaining social acceptance may override moral awareness under these circumstances.

Further still, it has also been suggested by offenders with a learning disability that their day-to-day life is much easier in a prison setting, as they receive the practical support for daily living which is so absent 'outside' in the community. It has long been argued that there is a lack of resources to fully support people with learning disabilities in the community, particularly those within a borderline range, and this could even in itself become a direct cause of 'criminal' behaviour. An example of this could be a person with a learning disability not understanding how to, or the need to, pay a fine. The implications of this could then become very serious, but could so easily have been prevented with some very simple practical input.

The prosecution process

Owing to their difficulty in understanding, people with a learning disability may have disastrous misunderstandings of what is being asked of them by the police, or in court. This naturally poses the question of what would constitute a fair trial. Reasonable steps and adjustments must be taken, particularly in court, to facilitate a person with learning disabilities' understanding. However, the real obstacle is being able to identify the person with a learning disability in the first place.

As with autism, a learning disability can be invisible and efforts are sometimes made by a person with a learning disability to mask their misunderstanding and confusion. This could be due to intense embarrassment, an unfamiliarity with having their own voice heard, or it could be due to their initial difficulty in consequential thinking in not fully acknowledging the implications their purposeful masking might have.

The overshadowing of difficulties

People with learning disabilities can often experience mental health issues, and have been argued to be more likely to experience such issues than people without a learning disability. This may be due to difficulties in problem solving, particularly in the face of intense emotions, where there is a lack of effective emotional regulation and control of subsequent impulsive behaviour. However, the difficulty in supporting people with learning disabilities who have mental illness lies within the identification of such difficulties, as it is common that a learning disability may overshadow a mental health issue, and vice versa. Presenting as a relatively understudied area of overshadowing, it is also being questioned if offending behaviour may mask learning disability needs, and again, vice versa. To overcome such issues of overshadowing requires an alertness and attentiveness to small indicators, and maintaining an awareness that such overshadowing may be at play.

Suggestions for good practice

There are some steps that could be taken which may prove beneficial in supporting people with autism and/or learning disabilities during their journey throughout the CJS. In an ideal context, it is hoped that a level of psychological therapy may be offered to such a forensic population. Psychological therapy may prove useful in encouraging understanding in emotional regulation strategies, consequential thinking, and interpersonal skills, which may be particularly helpful in raising awareness of exploitative social risks.

On a more general note, there are various simple steps that may be taken by a variety of professions, to encourage a more positive journey through the criminal justice system for people with autism and/or learning disabilities. These are outlined below:

Specific to learning disability
→ **Building social support**

Where possible, positive and pro-social connections should be built around people with learning disabilities, where they can develop a sense of belonging within social groups. Within such groups, the likelihood of exploitation and criminal coercion is hopefully reduced. In addition, with strong social connections, there is less room for people with learning disabilities' deviant behaviours going unnoticed and unmanaged.

→ **Ensuring meaning and understanding is shared**

Even if understanding appears clear, and shared, it is good practice to be thorough in checking that people with learning disabilities have understood you, and you them. Through simply asking people to share their understanding of what you have said, and regularly reflecting back your understanding of what they have said, the risk of becoming engrossed in a false or misinterpreted account could be reduced.

→ **Using visual means**

It would appear that people with learning disabilities might have difficulty with the exchange of information verbally on some occasions. Therefore, the use of more visual means to exchange information may be helpful in securing accurate information. For example, producing visual timelines, drawings detailing a sequence of events etc.

→ **Practical support**

Wherever possible, practical support should be provided to people with learning disabilities. This could take the form of various inputs, from being supported with general life skills in finding paid employment and paying bills, to support in their reading of prison rules. This is an aspect that would be particularly significant when supporting a person with learning disabilities in court, in having people explain to them complicated matters in lay terms, and offering support in their understanding and navigation through the court processes.

→ **Useful aspects to note for identification**

As previously noted, identifying a person with a learning disability can be difficult, particularly to those who have not been trained in such matters. To aid this identification, questions around a person's history could be asked, such as the school they may have attended. Was it a specialist school? In addition, you may want to ask what support they receive generally. Do they have a social worker? Some people may already be known to services regarding their learning disability. Wherever there is doubt over a person's capacity, psychological consultation should always be sought to gain clarification, to avoid damaging assumptions being made.

Specific to autism
→ Encourage the carrying of 'autism alert cards' to be presented to first responders.

→ Train staff within the police force and CJS in understanding autism.

→ Have specialist staff who have an academic qualification in autism.

→ Identify when an individual will require additional support as a vulnerable person.

→ Identify appropriate sensory spaces for autistic individuals in custody.

→ Have a range of communication methods on offer rather than just face-to-face interview/examinations throughout the systems.

→ Use autism specialists as expert witnesses where possible to enable a better understanding of events.

→ Increase understanding throughout the CJS in relation to the Equality Act and what reasonable adjustments might be required on an individual basis.

→ Promote an understanding of the model of disadvantage for autistic individuals.

References

Beardon L (2008) *Asperger Syndrome and Perceived Offending Conduct: A qualitative study.* Doctoral, Sheffield Hallam University.

Beardon (2017) *Autism and Asperger Syndrome in Adulthood.* London: Sheldon Press.

British Psychological Society (2000) *Learning Disability: Definitions and contexts.* Leicester: Professional Affairs Board of the British Psychological Society.

Kenny L, Hattersley C, Molins B, Buckley C, Povey C & Pellicano E (2016) Which terms should be used to describe autism? Perspectives from the UK autism community. *Autism: The International Journal of Research and Practice* **20** (4) 442–462

Milton D (2012) On the ontological status of autism: the 'double empathy problem'. *Disability and Society* **27** (6) 883–887.

Additional reading

Foster R (2014) Does the Equality Act 2010 ensure equality for individuals with Asperger syndrome in the legal arena? A survey of recent UK case law. *Autonomy, the Critical Journal of Interdisciplinary Autism Studies* **1** (4).

Parsons S & Sherwood G (2016) Vulnerability in custody: perceptions and practices of police officers and criminal justice professionals in meeting the communication needs of offenders with learning disabilities and learning difficulties. *Disability & Society* **31** (4) 553–572.

Poynter J (2011) People with learning disabilities who come in contact with the criminal justice system. *Tizard Learning Disability Review* **16** (2) 49–53.

The use of spit hoods by the police on autistic suspects

Kleio Cossburn

Abstract

The aim of this article is to investigate the appropriateness of using spit hoods by the police on autistic suspects. It has evaluated the strengths and weaknesses of 'spit hoods', considering the impact of their use on individuals diagnosed with autism. The results of the research indicate that using spit hoods on autistic suspects can cause physical pain and significant distress. Moreover, the findings suggest that some police forces in the UK have not been trained to identify suspects with a diagnosis of autism. This can lead to miscommunications and misinterpretations of suspects' behaviours. Spit hoods are applied if the suspect has a history of spitting or biting; therefore, their use may not be justified until after the suspect has spat at an officer. Thus, further research is required to establish alternative protection for police officers.

Background

The Diagnostic and Statistical Manual Fifth edition (DSM-5) defines autism as a lifelong developmental disability, which impacts on the individual's perceptions and social interactions with other people. Additionally, a person with diagnosis of an autism spectrum disorder presents with 'restricted and repetitive patterns of behaviours, activities or interests' (National Autistic Society, 2017).

Whilst it is estimated that only 1% of the population worldwide is autistic (Brugha et al, 2012), it has been reported by Browning and Caulfield (2008) that autistic people will come into contact with the criminal justice system significantly more often than non-autistic individuals. Statistically, autistic people are seven times more likely to be arrested (Curry et al, 1993). Despite this fact, Cheely et al (2012) reported lower rates of criminal charges of autistic young people compared to non-autistic youth. Nevertheless, there has been little analysis of these figures to provide an explanation. What is interesting, however, is that following a Freedom of Information Request in 2016, the data collected suggest that police forces across the UK have little or no training in autism awareness. To date, there appears to be a lack of empirical research that investigates if there is a correlation between a lack of autism awareness amongst police officers, and the higher number of arrest rates of autistic people. This is an important subject for future research. Nevertheless, research has been carried out on mental health training for police officers. It was suggested that officers trained in mental health awareness were less likely to use force on people having a mental health crisis than those officers who had not received training (Canada et al, 2011).

Whilst contact with the police may not be a positive experience for non-autistic people, the communication difficulties[1] autistic people experience may cause heightened anxieties during encounters with the police (Chown, 2010). This could lead to misunderstandings between the police and the autistic person. It has been suggested by Murray et al (2005) that some autistic people can only process one sensory channel at a time. For example, if they focus on visual information, they are unable to process auditory information. Therefore, any verbal requests may not be responded to and this may be misinterpreted by police officers as non-compliance and resisting arrest, which could then result in force being used. This, in turn, may cause a 'fright or flight' reaction in some autistic people, specifically those who are hypersensitive to touch where the lightest touch can cause physical pain (Bogdashina & Lawson, 2003). It is well documented that autistic people's sensory sensitivity was first identified by Kanner (1943) and Asperger (Frith, 1994), who both described unusual reactions by their patients to sensory stimuli. Pellicano and Burr (2012) suggest that it is the way in which autistic people perceive sensory stimuli that causes the problems associated with sensory sensitivity. Therefore, using a spit hood on an autistic person could result in physical pain and a 'fright or flight' response, as previously discussed.

Spit hoods

Since 2016, there has been an increase in the introduction of spit hoods[2] across police forces in the UK. They are slowly being introduced as part of a police officer's personal protective equipment (PPE) and consequently, they will become standard issue for some front-line officers (Dodd, 2016). The application of spit hoods on suspects is considered a use of force governed by Section 3 of the Criminal Law Act (1967). This means that a police officer may use reasonable force to prevent a crime, or in the effecting or assisting in the lawful arrest of offenders or a suspected offender, as per the act. Therefore, the 'National Decision

---

1 There is agreement that autism involves delays in three particular areas of function (often referred to as the triad of impairment) i.e. socialisation, communication, and imagination (Chown, 2010).
2 Spit hoods are mesh fabric hoods placed over the heads of suspects to prevent spitting or biting.

Model[3] should be considered, which means that the decision made to use the spit hood has to be justifiable. A key example of justifiable using the National Decision Model would be when the suspect has previously spat at an officer or a member of the public, or if the officer perceives a threat that the suspect will spit (British Transport Police, n.d.).

Whilst autism is not recorded separately on custody records it has been established that 39% of people detained by the police are considered to be mentally vulnerable (National Institute for Health and Care Excellence, 2017). It has been reported that since 2011 spit hoods have been used on suspects at least 2,486 times, of which 635 were people suffering from mental health issues and 91 cases were reported to have involved children under 18 years old (Bakes, 2016). In this case Code C of the Police and Criminal Evidence Act (PACE) (1984) states that care must be taken if deciding to use restraints within cells, including spit hoods, on mentally disordered or otherwise mentally vulnerable detainees, such as people with learning disabilities and/or autism.

There have been a number of cases publicised where police have used force on autistic people. One particular example of this is a case where Sussex police were referred to the Independent Police Complaints Commission for using spit hood on an 11-year-old autistic girl. It was found that the officers failed to record their rationale for using the spit hood (Independent Police Complaints Commission, 2016). Another example is the case of ZH v The Commissioner of Police for the Metropolis (2012), where officers restrained a 16-year-old autistic boy. The findings of this case showed officers acted hastily in restraining ZH. Despite these documented cases where inappropriate force was used by police officers on autistic people and other vulnerable suspects, there has been little discussion about the use of spit hoods on vulnerable suspects, such as those with a diagnosis of autism.

Risk assessment

Public Health England (2014) established that 8% of the prison population, in comparison with 2% of general primary care, have a diagnosis of hepatitis C. Notably, 50% of drug users that inject drugs test positive for hepatitis C. This percentage is higher in London where 59% of drug users test positive (ibid). In addition to the increase of cases of hepatitis C within the prison population, there is also a significant increase in drug resistant tuberculosis (TB) amongst those considered to have a social risk factor. Social risk factors include a history of drug and alcohol misuse, homelessness, and people within the criminal justice system (Public Health England, 2016). The results of the data collected by Public Health England (2016) showed that TB is more prevalent in the following police force areas: Thames Valley, Leicestershire, West Midlands, Bedfordshire, Lancashire, and Greater Manchester. Interestingly, Bedfordshire (Geoghegan, 2016) and Thames Valley (Hickey, 2017) are the only forces currently issuing spit hoods to all front-line police officers. Therefore, the police forces in other higher risk areas are not protected from contracting TB if a suspect with TB was to spit at them.

On the other hand, according to Merchant et al (2008), police officers are less likely to be exposed to blood-borne viruses than other emergency services, such as paramedics, who are not issued with spit hoods. Nevertheless, Geoghegan (2016), from the Centre of Public Safety, proposes that the risk of catching a blood-borne disease through an assault of spitting or biting is substantially higher for police officers than other emergency services. Geoghegan points out the encounters that the police have with individuals are often confrontational and more volatile, suggesting that an individual with hepatitis C, or HIV, or TB may use their disease as a weapon. This could be achieved by deliberately self-harming to produce blood in their phlegm (ibid). This was the case in 2015 when a 20-year-old female with hepatitis B, which is also a blood-borne virus, was being arrested for public order offences. She deliberately bit her lip and then spat at officers. Consequently, three police officers were taken to hospital and treated with anti-viral medication (Alwakeel, 2015).

What we do know, from a Freedom of Information Request (no. 41098) to the Home Office, is that the Centre for Applied Science and Technology (CAST) has not formally evaluated spit hoods. Moreover, CAST have not yet identified suitable models for use (Home Office, 2016). This would suggest that alternatives, such as safety glasses, which are used by police officers in Essex, might not have been considered (Halliday et al, 2016). Whilst safety glasses would not protect an officer from being bitten, they would prevent saliva from entering the eyes; thus, offering some protection similar to that of spit hood. Additionally, safety glasses used by the officer do not require justification for their use, unlike a spit hood. Safety glasses would also mean that vulnerable suspects, such as those diagnosed with autism, are not distressed further by the application of a spit hood.

Conclusion

Consequently, the protection of one group of people, namely the police, may create the potential for harm to a second group – i.e. those considered as vulnerable. As such, the use of spit hoods may be considered a more complex situation, and policies or actions which may potentially cause harm to a member of the public. Using a spit hood on an autistic person that has a hypersensitivity to touch may be harmful, both physically and mentally. Therefore, de-escalating the situation would be a more desirable approach than using a spit hood. Training of police officers is required to enable them to recognise autistic suspects and communicate with them appropriately to reduce the risk of causing distress. More research is necessary to examine the long-term efficacy and safety of spit hoods, especially when they are used on autistic people.

References

Alwakeel R (2015) *Three Police Officers Taken To Hospital After 'Hepatitis B Sufferer Spits Blood in their Faces'* [online] Available at: http://www.standard.co.uk/news/london/three-police-officers-taken-to-hospital-after-hepatitis-b-sufferer-spits-blood-in-their-faces-10279070.html (accessed September 2017).

---

3 The National Decision Model has six key elements: codes of ethics, information and intelligence gathering, assessment of threat and risk, powers and policies, options, action and review. The police codes of ethics are at the centre of all police decision making (College of Policing 2017).

Bakes C (2016) *Cruel Spit Hoods Used by Third of UK Police Forces* [online]. Police Community Magazine. Available at: http://police.community/topic/92614-bbc-cruel-spit-hoods-used-by-third-of-uk-police-forces/ (accessed September 2017).

Bogdashina O and Lawson W (2003) *Sensory Perceptual Issues in Autism: Different sensory experiences – different perceptual worlds*. London: Jessica Kingsley Publishers.

British Transport Police (nd) *FOI Response 980-16 Spit Hoods Guidance Document* [online]. Available at: https://www.btp.police.uk/pdf/FOI%20Response%20980-16%20Spit%20Hoods%20Doc%202%20BTP%20Guidance%20Document.pdf (accessed September 2017).

Browning A and Caulfield L (2011) The prevalence and treatment of people with Asperger's Syndrome in the criminal justice system. *Journal of Criminology and Criminal Justice* **11** (2) 165–180.

Brugha T, Cooper SA, McManus S, Purdon S, Smith J, Scott FJ, Spiers N & Tyrer F (2012) *Estimating the Prevalence of Autism Spectrum Conditions in Adults: Extending the 2007 adult psychiatric morbidity survey*. Leeds: NHS Information Centre for Health and Social Care.

Canada KE, Angell B & Watson AC (2011) Intervening at the entry point: differences in how CIT trained and non-CIT trained officers describe responding to mental health-related calls. *Community Mental Health Journal* **48** (6) 746–755.

Cheely CA, Carpenter LA, Letourneau EJ, Nicholas, JS, Charles J & King LB (2012) The prevalence of youth with autism spectrum disorders in the Criminal Justice System. *Journal of Autism & Developmental Disorders* **42** 1856–1862.

Chown N (2010) Do you have any difficulties I may not be aware of? A study of autism awareness and understanding in the UK service. *International Journal of Police Science & Management* **12** (2) 256–273.

College of Policing (2017) *National Decision Model* [online]. Available at: https://www.app.college.police.uk/app-content/national-decision-model/the-national-decision-model/#code-of-ethics (accessed September 2017).

Curry KL, Posluszny MP & Kraska SL (1993) Training criminal justice personnel to recognize offenders with disabilities. *OSERS News in Print* **5** (3) 4–8.

Dodd V (2016) *Met Police to Start Using Spit Hoods on Suspects Within Weeks.* [online]. Available at: https://www.theguardian.com/uk-news/2016/sep/06/met-police-to-start-using-spit-hoods-on-suspects-within-weeks (accessed September 2017).

Frith U (1994) *Autism and Asperger Syndrome*. Cambridge: Cambridge University Press.

Geoghegan R (2016) *Spit Guards: A protective and preventative measure that is overdue* [online]. Available at: https://www.centreforpublicsafety.com/2016/09/spit-guards-a-protective-and-preventative-measure-that-is-overdue/ (accessed September 2017).

Halliday J, Grierson J & Nugent C (2016) *UK Police Forces Under Pressure to Stop Using Spit Hoods* [online]. Available at: https://www.theguardian.com/law/2016/aug/29/uk-police-forces-under-pressure-to-stop-using-spit-hoods (accessed September 2017).

Hickey H (2017) *Forces Introduce Spit Hoods for all Frontline Officers*. [online]. Available at: http://www.policeoracle.com/news/Spitting-risk-to-officers-'overinflated',-says-charity_94247.html (accessed September 2017).

Home Office (2016) *The Centre for Applied Science and Technology (CAST) Evaluation and Assessment of Spit Hoods and Guards* [online]. Available at: https://www.whatdotheyknow.com/request/the_centre_for_applied_science_a#incoming-875314 (accessed September 2017).

Independent Police Complaints Commission (2016) *IPCC Recommends Sussex Police Makes Improvements after 11-year-old Disabled Girl Held in Cells Overnight* [online]. Available at: https://www.ipcc.gov.uk/news/ipcc-recommends-sussex-police-makes-improvements-after-11-year-old-disabled-girl-held-cells (accessed September 2017).

Kanner L (1943) Autistic disturbances of affective contact. *Nervous Child* **2** 217–250.

Merchant RC, Nettleton JE, Mayer KH, Becker BM. (2008). HIV post-exposure prophylaxis among police and corrections officers. *Occupational Medicine* **58**:502–505

Murray D, Lesser M, Lawson W (2005) Attention, monotropism and the diagnostic criteria for autism. *Autism* **9** (2) 139–156.

National Autistic Society (2017) *Autism: A guide for police officers and staff*. London: National Autistic Society.

National Institute for Health and Care Excellence (2017) *Mental Health of Adults in Contact with the Criminal Justice System* [online]. Available at: https://www.nice.org.uk/guidance/ng66/evidence/full-guideline-4419120205?utm_content=buffer6bc80&utm_medium=social&utm_source=twitter.com&utm_campaign=buffer (accessed September 2017).

Pellicano E and Burr D (2012) When the world becomes too real: a bayesian explanation of autistic perception. *Trends in Cognitive Science* **16** (10) 504–510.

Public Health England (2014) *No Health Without Justice, No Justice Without Help* [online]. Available at: https://www.gov.uk/government/uploads/system/uploads/attachment_data/file/562775/Health_and_justice_report_2014.PDF (accessed September 2017).

Public Health England (2016) *Tuberculosis in England: 2016 report* [online]. Available at: https://www.gov.uk/government/uploads/system/uploads/attachment_data/file/581238/TB_Annual_Report_2016_GTW2309_errata_v1.2.pdf (accessed September 2017).

ZH v The Commissioner of Police for the Metropolis (2012) EWHC 604 (QB).

Accessible information within the criminal justice system

Professor Sarah Parsons

Abstract

A high number of offenders within the criminal justice system are known to have learning difficulties or disabilities. The criminal justice system is very paper-based, which can make information and processes very difficult to understand for many people. Accessible information has a role to play within this context, both as a way of presenting information in a different format and also as means of mediating discussions. This paper presents an overview of a study that piloted a symbol-based rights and entitlements form in custody. The form was positively received by custody personnel, who also reported positive responses from individuals entering custody.

Introduction

Approximately 20-30% of all offenders in the UK have learning difficulties or learning disabilities, which can make the very difficult environment of the criminal justice system (CJS) even harder to navigate (Jacobson, 2008). Here, the term 'learning disabilities' is used to refer to people with an intellectual impairment, which may be severe, while 'learning difficulties' is a broader term that covers people with a range of comprehension, cognitive, and communication difficulties including dyslexia, dyspraxia, autism, and language impairments. Meeting the needs of individuals with intellectual impairments or learning difficulties within the CJS can be very challenging; for example offenders with intellectual impairments are more likely to be restrained or isolated in prison and to be excluded from programmes that may help them to address problems associated with being incarcerated (Prison Reform Trust, 2013). In addition, prisoners with learning difficulties or disabilities report high levels of bullying and abuse and this is a major cause for concern (Talbot, 2010).

Despite appearances or implications in the media, there is no evidence to suggest that autistic individuals are overrepresented within the CJS (King & Murphy, 2014). However some argue that associated with autism are certain 'predisposing features' (King & Murphy, 2014; p2717) that may lead individuals towards committing a crime, and once within the CJS, finding the context and procedures particularly difficult (Chown, 2010; Allen et al, 2008). Such apparent 'predisposing features' include:

→ Cognitive difficulties relating to understanding non-literal language and interpreting the intentions and behaviours of other people, potentially leading to vulnerability to exploitation by other people.

→ Sensory difficulties relating to lights, sounds and smells which may result in high anxiety and possibly a public meltdown which could, in turn, be characterised by others as an aggressive outburst.

→ Social and communication difficulties which can exacerbate already tense situations, particularly if other people react in an adverse or aversive manner thus making things worse.

→ Adherence to routines or rituals which, if disrupted, may lead to seemingly 'aggressive' behaviours, which the author would again classify as meltdowns rather than intentional aggression.

Police and custody officers often lack skills and awareness in the identification of alleged offenders with learning difficulties or disabilities or mental health difficulties and, therefore, require more training in these areas in order to avoid making things worse (Bradley, 2009).

The problem with written information in the CJS

A reliance on written communication creates particular problems for many people with learning difficulties or disabilities within the CJS. For an alleged offender who may have difficulties with reading and/or writing, navigating and understanding the systems of the CJS can be a significant challenge. For example, Talbot (2010) interviewed 154 prisoners with learning difficulties or disabilities and found that over two-thirds reported challenges with reading and completing written forms and information within the CJS. In some cases, there is the potential for miscarriages of justice because individuals may not understand why they have been arrested, cautioned, or held in custody (Jones & Talbot, 2010).

One of the most crucial times when someone needs to understand their rights is at the point of arrest and when being taken into custody. By law everyone in this situation must be provided with written information that explains their 'rights and entitlements' while in custody, including the provision of food and drink, medical attention, reasonable standards for physical comfort, circumstances when an appropriate adult can assist, the conduct of interviews, and how to make a complaint. This information, at least in England, is currently supplied via a folded leaflet with small and densely worded text (see **Figure 1**), and is available in 54 different languages (see link in the Useful Resources section for access to these leaflets).

Reviews of communication practices within the CJS have recommended that improvements need to be made to how information is provided to alleged offenders and inmates (Jacobson, 2008). As a result, the rights and entitlements notice is also available in an Easy Read format, which uses short and simple words and pictures to present this information. Such formats can be helpful for aiding comprehension of information, though the booklet is 33 pages long and there has been no published evaluation of using this version in custody. Therefore, it is not clear how many people have received it or how helpful it is. Other examples of Easy Read information for the CJS can be found in the Useful Resources at the end of this chapter.

The potential of using symbol-based information in custody: a case study

A different way of making information more accessible for people who may struggle to read or understand written texts is through the use of symbol communication (e.g. Widgit Symbols and Picture Communication Symbols (PCS)). Research findings are mixed as to whether the use of symbols can improve comprehension of information, however symbols can help to meet the information needs of individuals, depending on their motivations and previous experiences, as well as the context in which communication takes place (see Parsons & Sherwood (2015) listed in Useful Resources for a summary of the research in this area).

A small-scale project was carried out in Hampshire to investigate the feasibility of using a more accessible rights and entitlements notice using Widgit symbols and simple text (Parsons & Sherwood, 2016a; 2016b). As one of the first, formal, paper-based processes that individuals experience when they enter the CJS, this presents an opportunity to make a positive change at one of the earliest possible occasions. The idea for the sheets came from a custody nurse who approached Autism Hampshire and asked if the organisation could support her work to develop a custody sheet to support her client base. Although the Easy Read version of the rights and entitlements notice was available, this had not proved very helpful in practice.

Given the known difficulties of identifying the needs of people coming into custody, the symbol-based custody leaflets were not intended to be autism specific and custody teams were asked to use their discretion by giving the Widgit version (**Figure 2**) to '…anyone who you think may be vulnerable or have difficulties communicating and understanding' (Parsons & Sherwood, 2016a; 2016b). They gave out the symbol-based leaflet in addition to the 'standard' rights and entitlements notice (**Figure 1**). Further information using the symbol format was also provided in a separate folder, which contained

individual laminated sheets regarding specific aspects of processes and procedures such as 'If you are ill' and 'Your DNA'. The Widgit Symbol custody leaflets were piloted in two custody centres in Hampshire for a period of four weeks.

Feedback on the usefulness of the Widgit Symbol information in custody

Feedback about the Widgit leaflets was obtained from 41 people in total. This number included 14 custody personnel who had used the information during the pilot study, plus different stakeholders from the CJS, and the wider

Figure 1: Standard rights and entitlements notice given when entering custody following an arrest (reproduced with permission from Widgit Software)

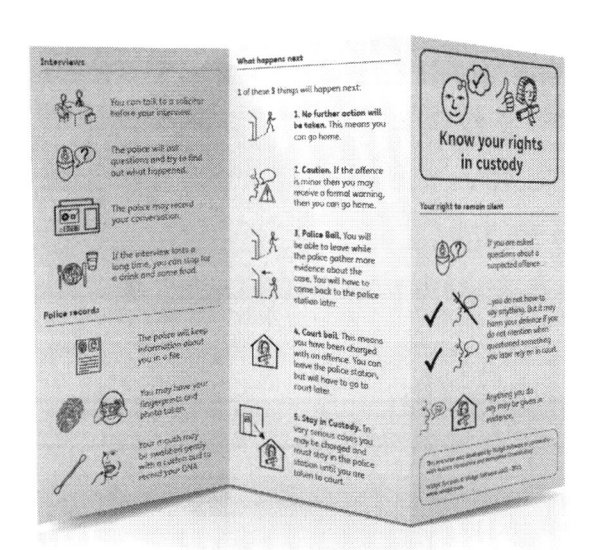

Figure 2: Widgit Symbol rights and entitlements notice (reproduced with permission from Widgit Software)

community. The stakeholders included: young people on the autism spectrum and their families, people with intellectual impairments, 'appropriate adults', and senior personnel within the CJS (e.g. solicitors, magistrates). No offenders were observed during the pilot implementation so there was no direct evaluation of the use of the Widgit Symbol information with offenders within a custody context.

There were some very encouraging findings from the pilot study: custody personnel who used the symbol-based leaflets with some people entering custody were very positive about providing information in this format. Most of the people interviewed thought that the symbol-based leaflets were a good idea because they helped to make information more accessible for those who needed this. Many participants felt that the symbol-based leaflets would be useful for a wide range of people entering custody, and used words such as 'reassuring', 'friendly', 'accessible', and 'engaging' to describe the Widgit symbol notice. The following comment sums up why this format of the information could be useful:

'… just a skim read of it clearly shows that for some of our young people this is far more accessible than this. For me as well it's far more accessible… it's been developed… with autism in mind but diagrams, figures like this, that would be useful for unaccompanied asylum seekers for example who don't have a full understanding of English, people with general learning difficulties, people who are visual learners talking earlier about our learning styles assessments. It's got … the potential to be invaluable in all sorts of different areas.'
(Manager of a youth offending team)

Indeed, one of the recommendations from the project was that the symbol-based information should be given to everyone entering custody so that there is no need for custody personnel to try to distinguish between those who may have difficulties with accessing information in standard ways, and those who do not.

Comments from two of the autistic young people (aged 13-15 years) reinforced the view that the symbol-based information seemed to be more accessible on a very practical level compared to with the larger (33-page) Easy Read version from the Home Office:

'I think it's good because the pictures aren't as detailed they are more like clearer, than they are not as distracting… I like the fact that there aren't loads of pages to read through, it's just like a little thing you can read a page at a time.'
(Female)

'I think it's good because you feel like you've got a lot less to read when you're handed this [symbol leaflet], *extremely light compared to this* [Easy Read version].*'*
(Male)

The size of the symbol version was also considered helpful as this custody officer suggests:

' … the fact that it's sort of pocket size, you can fold that and put it in your pocket and draw on it again whereas most of the forms are A4… this they might well put it in their pocket and keep it as sort of a guide if you like.'

Many participants also highlighted the importance of consistency in where and how symbol-based information might be used in the CJS, for example, in all custody centres, the courts, prison, and within the probation service). It was emphasised by some that the symbol-based information should not be seen as a replacement for verbal interaction and support with helping the detained person to understand what was happening to them. A limitation of this small-scale study was the lack of feedback about the symbol-based information from, or observations of, offenders with learning disabilities or difficulties. This is clearly a very important area for future research. Overall however, the fact that the symbol-based information was so positively received by participants with very different roles and perspectives on the CJS suggest that this more accessible format could have an important role to play in the provision of information in the CJS in the future.

References

Allen D, Evans C, Hider A, Hawkins S, Peckett H & Morgan H (2008) Offending behaviour in adults with Asperger syndrome. Journal of *Autism and Developmental Disorders* **38** (4) 748–758.

Bradley K (2009) *The Bradley Report: Lord Bradley's review of people with mental health problems or learning disabilities in the criminal justice system* [online]. Available at: http://www.prisonreformtrust.org.uk/ProjectsResearch/Mentalhealth/TroubledInside/BradleyReport (accessed September 2017).

Chown N (2010) 'Do you have any difficulties that I may not be aware of?' A study of autism awareness and understanding in the UK police service. *International Journal of Police Science & Management* **12** (2) 256–273.

Jacobson J (2008) *No One Knows: Police responses to suspect's learning disabilities and learning difficulties: A review of policy and practice* [online]. Prison Reform Trust (PRT). Available at: http://www.prisonreformtrust.org.uk/Publications/vw/1/ItemID/88 (accessed September 2017).

Jones G & Talbot J (2010) Editorial - no one knows: the bewildering passage of offenders with learning disability and learning difficulty through the criminal justice system. *Criminal Behaviour and Mental Health* **20** (1) 1–7.

King C & Murphy GH (2014) A systematic review of people with autism spectrum disorder and the criminal justice system. *Journal of Autism and Developmental Disorders* **44** (11) 2717–2733.

Parsons S & Sherwood G (2016a) Vulnerability in custody: perceptions and practices of police officers and criminal justice professionals in meeting the communication needs of offenders with learning disabilities and learning difficulties. *Disability & Society* **31** (4) 553–572.

Parsons S & Sherwood G (2016b) A pilot evaluation of using symbol-based information in police custody. *British Journal of Learning Disabilities* **44** (3) 213–224.

Prison Reform Trust (2013) *Prison: The facts – Bromley briefings summer 2013* [online]. Available at: http://www.prisonreformtrust.org.uk/Portals/0/Documents/Prisonthefacts.pdf (accessed September 2017).

Talbot J (2010) Prisoners' voices: experiences of the criminal justice system by prisoners with learning disabilities. *Tizard Learning Disability Review* **15** (3) 33–41.

Useful resources

→ The full research report on The Widgit Symbol Custody Sheet Pilot Project by Sarah Parsons and Gina Sherwood (2015): www.widgit.com/custodysheets.

→ Examples of other Easy Read materials used within the CJS: http://www.keyring.org/cjs-easyreadexamples.

→ The Home Office (2014) versions of the rights and entitlements notice in Easy Read format and different languages: https://www.gov.uk/guidance/notice-of-rights-and-entitlements-a-persons-rights-in-police-detention.

→ Other examples of Widgit symbols being used to support understanding in other contexts:

   → The production of materials and activities for the English National Ballet to make ballet more accessible to children with learning difficulties and disabilities: http://www.widgit.com/resources/popular-topics/myfirstballet/index.htm.

   → A range of health-related resources for children and adults: http://widgit-health.com/downloads/.

Autism, intellectual impairment and old age

Professor Nicola Martin and Joanna Krupa

Abstract

There is very little research about autism and intellectual impairment in later life, and it is of concern to autistic people and their families that there is no obvious source of advice about high quality services dedicated to ensuring that life can be lived to the full right up until death. Advanced planning is clearly a good idea, but looking into what might be out there can feel like staring into a void and this can create anxiety for those trying to plan ahead. This anxiety is well founded, as provision is limited and there seems to be little political will to change this situation, despite equalities and autism legislation which aims to improve quality of life for autistic and other disabled people throughout life. The picture is worrying for those who are formally diagnosed and there will also inevitably be ageing adults on the spectrum who never had the opportunity to access a diagnosis and the notional legal protections this may afford. Some generic information about medical, social, emotional and practical aspects of ageing may be useful, but it is essential to think specifically about what might be helpful for older autistic people with lifelong or acquired cognitive difficulties and who may also experience lifelong or acquired barriers to communication. Understanding autism from a social model perspective is important, but the emphasis must be place on individuality, so that professionals are alive to potential stereotyping, including making heteronormative assumptions. Listening to autistic people about this subject provides a good starting point, and more autistic involvement in research about what might be conducive to health and happiness in old age, and the deployment of resources to make this happen would be marvellous.

Introduction

The lack of research into services to assist autistic older people has been highlighted by the National Autistic Society (NAS) and others (Barber, 2015; Bennett, 2016; McPartland et al, 2015; Michael, 2016; Piven & Rabins, 2011). Although there is a body of research about acquired cognitive impairment alongside the development of conditions such as dementia and Alzheimer's, there is very little which focuses on the lives of people for whom lifelong intellectual impairment has been a reality. There is even less relating to the geriatric requirements of people with autism and (acquired or lifelong) intellectual impairment together. No volume about autism and intellectual impairment in adulthood would be complete without thinking about the whole adult life span. Given the flimsy evidence base on which to draw, this article attempts to articulate some key principles and areas for future research.

We will all get old if we live long enough. This paper does not provide a numerical definition of later life because individuals experience the limitations of old age and require additional support accordingly at different stages in their life course depending on various factors including fitness and levels of activity and community participation. Attributing an arbitrary number to this would be unhelpful, although milestones such as retirement and the death of parents can be useful life course markers as they may signal points at which requirements for assistance change, and something for which advanced planning would make sense.

With ageing comes cognitive, health, physical and emotional changes which are quite individual and need to be understood by those around us and by professionals who may be delivering services on which we may come to rely. Autistic people are no exception of course, (Lever et al, 2016; Totskia et al, 2010), and additional considerations may need to be taken into account alongside those typically associated with later life. While an understanding of autism, from a social model perspective, will be helpful for service providers, this only creates a backdrop against which to develop an understanding of the individual with all their unique hopes, dreams and aspirations. If you have met one (older) autistic person, you have met one (older) autistic person.

The NAS's 2013 campaign *Getting On: Growing Older with Autism* reminds us that 'Ageing people need to be able to talk about their health'. We extend the notion to health and well-being, encompassing physical and mental health and individual interests, passions, relationships and everything else that makes life rich and fulfilling. The NAS campaign goes on to suggest that 'If professionals learn as much as they can about the person they support, they are more likely to spot changes in behaviour or mannerisms which may signal that the person with autism is having problems'. The NAS acknowledges that 'talk' will not necessarily be the primary mode of communication for some autistic people, particularly those with additional intellectual impairments. Finding out about the wants and needs in old age of those for whom communication has never been easy, requires some effort and may well involve engaging with people who are close to the individual with autism or have known them for a long time.

It is possible that additional communication challenges may develop in old age as a consequence of, for example, having a stroke. It is also possible that a very elderly parent has been the conduit to communication for an individual for all their life and this is something that could come to an abrupt halt if the parent dies or acquires age-related communication difficulties themselves. Any situation which relies on a very old person caring for an old person without support is obviously not sustainable, but that does not mean that it does not happen. Reliable figures are not available as families can be below the radar, particularly if they have 'always just managed' and not accessed services before. It is quite possible that the autistic person is not diagnosed.

We must not fall into the trap of assuming that it is always the autistic person who is the recipient of care from another family member. Ageing autistic carers receive no research attention and we must acknowledge their existence. Autistic parents of autistic children may find themselves in this position later, and sensitive support with forward planning may be needed. Without a crystal ball it is not possible to say what sort of assistance will be out there in the future so it would be wise to engage with autistic parents as co-researchers right now on this subject.

We have no accurate information about how many old people are on the autism spectrum. Wallace et al (2016) remind us that it was not until the 1940s that the first generation of children were to receive an autism diagnosis and it is therefore only relatively recently that these individuals are moving into old age. Some will not have accessed formal schooling (D'Astous et al, 2014). More recently still, diagnosis in adulthood has increased and it is likely that there are many more autistic adults around who have not had access to any formal diagnostic process. Although there is some evidence of premature mortality for people with intellectual impairments (Public Health England, 2014), it is safe to assume that the majority of people with autism will live to an age at which some form of geriatric support will be required. Articulate adults on the spectrum are expressing a degree of concern about what old age might look like for them without any obvious focus on ensuring that services are designed with autistic elderly people in mind. 'Knowing that there is such a paucity of research about supporting us as we grow older makes old age a frightening prospect' (Michael, 2016, p515). Research into old age involving autistic people who do not communicate verbally, whether or not they have additional intellectual impairments, is almost non-existent and therefore we will have to rely on that which is informed by autistic researchers who are able to empathise with many of the experiences of those who are silent.

Much of the research which is available tends to focus on the medical and health-related aspects of ageing, rather than, for example, the psychological and social changes. Focusing on health is of course important given the higher rates of poor health and mortality of adults with learning disabilities (Public Health England, 2014). People with intellectual impairments are eligible for an annual health check from their GP, and this should help to identify health needs more promptly than has often previously been the case. There is evidence to suggest that these health checks are not always taken up (Glover et al, 2013). Changes to the body and physical functioning need to be considered and discussed sensitively in ways which are appropriate to the individual and inclusive of people who do not use speech. For example, McCarthy and Millard (2003) attempted to explore the concept of menopause with a group of women with intellectual impairments, from the women's' own perspective, rather than just as a medical phenomenon. From working with advisory groups of learning disabled women, these researchers make useful suggestions around the importance of explaining what these changes in their bodies might mean, and then following this up with regular accessible reminders, which may employ the use of pictures, symbols and other aids to communication appropriately with the individual. Professionals would benefit from training in dealing with the subject sensitively, with respect for the individual underpinned by an understanding of autism from a social model perspective. Staff working with women should be prepared for discussion about the physical aspects of ageing around and after the menopause.

Topics such as loss, bereavement and sexuality also need to be considered without automatic heteronormative assumptions being made about the individual. (Milton's chapter on idealised normalcy in this issue unpacks the idea of normativity further. Heteronormativity is about the assumption that everyone is heterosexual). Bereavement extends beyond family relationships. An autistic person may have extremely close friends with whom their communication is largely via the internet. The death of such an important person should never be dismissed as of lesser significance because the relationship is poorly understood by service providers and others. Milton and Simms (2016) remind us of the importance of autistic company which enables some autistic people to be themselves without trying to fit in to neurotypical ways of being. Lots of those conversations take place online.

Many older people with intellectual impairments and autism have been cared for by family members, often parents (Bibby, 2012), who will obviously themselves be growing older. Inevitably this may lead to situations where extra support needs to be provided, possibly at a time of profound grief and upheaval when a caregiver dies. Recent publicity about abusive practices in social care, for example the Panorama documentary about Winterbourne View, will continue to lead to concerns for some families about engaging with services. This is one of many reasons (Bibby, 2012) why older people and their families may find it more difficult to consider future planning, which in turn can lead to crises in support; for example, if the carer of an autistic adult with intellectual impairment who has never previously received any external support is admitted to hospital or dies suddenly. There are however also instances where the adult with autism and intellectual impairments provides care for their older relative, and again, both parties may find it hard to accept changes in this situation. Other reasons which may be a barrier to future planning include difficult relationships with professionals, carers feeling there will be some loss of identity, and the obvious emotional difficulty in broaching this sensitive subject. Sometimes caring for the carer will enable families to stay together. The media occasionally highlights the sad situation of elderly married couples being separated when one person needs to go into residential care but it is very rare to hear about the grief and loss of identity experienced by elderly people who are removed from the person for whom they are caring, let alone the emotions which someone who does not communicate via speech may be feeling. It would be nice to imagine that the elderly carer and the person for whom they are caring could be provided with support which enables them to stay together for as long as possible, while in the background someone is empathically helping with the whole thorny issue of future planning. Waiting for a crisis and then trying to make a plan is obviously ridiculous and it is particularly important to remember that unpredictable unforeseen change is especially disruptive for autistic people.

There is some evidence to suggest that professionals have made assumptions about people from black and minority ethnic (BME) communities continuing to be supported by their extended families following the death of their parents, which has led to BME disabled people being less likely to receive services (Walker & Ward, 2013). Identity is multi-faceted, as The Equality Act (2010) reminds us. Service providers should not assume that all families originating from BME backgrounds have extended social support networks, or that everyone is heterosexual and gender conformist, or indeed that autistic people are asexual or, like Greta Garbo, just want to be alone. Stereotyping is problematic and creates barriers to getting to know the individual, their circumstances, wants, needs and passions.

It is clear that making assumptions about people's lifestyles as they age is not useful. In fact, for the women talking about menopause, some of them were very aware of discrimination or stigma they might face, and did not want to identify themselves as 'older' (McCarthy & Millard, 2003). Ageing does not automatically mean a reduction in activities, and many people will wish to continue living actively and socially. In some instances, older people who are placed in 'generic' residential elder care because of a health or mobility crisis, end up losing their independence. Previous services or support which enabled them to pursue their activities of choice are no longer funded, homes are not sufficiently staffed to facilitate continued community access, and people's lifestyles become more sedentary with the potential loss of skills and adverse effects on physical and mental health (Blackman, 2007).

Case study

Restricting access to the internet can severely impact on the social life of some autistic people who may have close friends with whom they communicate online. As a social worker, I (Joanna) was aware, for example, of a man whose health declined, although his cognitive abilities were intact. He was therefore moved to a residential home many miles from where he had lived all his life, but close to his sister, who was also ageing. However, the home did not fund staff to accompany him on visits, and it took several years for the funding to be agreed. In the meantime, his horizons were narrowed, due in part to the limitations of the home. A long, time consuming gap between policy and good practice can, as with this illustration, have devastating effects. While we do not have space to explore here the implication that this scenario arose as a result of how older people are perceived in general, and that this might be reflected in the resourcing of social care elder services, this concern is in our minds. Harbottle and Jones (2016) discussed compassion in social care in the first volume in this series. We are big fans of the notions of compassion, respect and dignity.

End of life care merits discussion. Public Health England's 2014 report, *Making Reasonable Adjustments to End of Life Care for People with Learning Disabilities*, including an Easy Read summary, gives useful case studies showing how agencies have worked to improve end of life care, and a comprehensive list of resources. There are also many examples of end of life plans online which can be used to ensure the wishes of autistic people and those with intellectual disabilities are carried out. Dunn (2016), in the first volume of this series, discussed the use of the Mental Capacity Act (2005), and advised that professionals, including medical staff, should ensure they are familiar with the act, and use it ethically to make sure that any decisions made about a person who lacks capacity are made in their best interests. This does not just apply to end of life care. Notionally, sensitive, dignified and compassionate use of the act would contribute to preventing situations such as one I (Joanna) was aware of, where it was discovered that a man with an intellectual impairment had a 'Do Not Resuscitate' instruction on his hospital file, without his consent or the knowledge of his circle of support. In such cases it is difficult not to infer that judgements have previously been made about quality of life (see also the CIPOLD report (Heslop *et al*, 2013)). Similarly, people with intellectual impairments have been less able to access palliative care services, (Public Health England, 2014) and this inequality also needs to be challenged under the Equality Act (2010), which numbers age and disability amongst its protected characteristics.

Recommendations

Research

→ More research, informed by autistic people, about the experiences, needs and wishes of people who do not use verbal communication, is essential.

→ Support is required for autistic adults with intellectual impairment, their carers and families, and people working with them, in discussing and planning for the future.

→ Research which identifies barriers which obstruct effective forward planning is necessary.

→ Further development of services which can meet the specific requirements of older autistic people with intellectual impairments is necessary, as the current 'generic' model often does not meet their needs, including palliative care services. Autistic people are best placed to advise on what this might look like.

Staying active in older age

As we get older, it is more important than ever to look after ourselves. Keeping active is one of the best ways of improving our physical and mental well-being. This information will be helpful to those who are not very active at the moment or are looking for ways of doing more. It's never too late to start making a change.

Being active in later life has many benefits for older adults with autism. Everyone with autism can:

→ improve their health, well-being and independence

→ keep in touch with their local community and friends

→ learn new things, maintain interests and enjoy life

→ use physical activity to help manage stress and anxiety.

If you are someone who supports a person with autism, physical activity will also make a difference to your quality of life as well. The benefits are there for everyone. For more information please see *A Practical Guide to Healthy Ageing* (NHS England & Age UK, 2015).

Health conditions and ageing

When a person has autism and any other mental or physical health condition, they are said to have a co-existing condition (e.g. depression, epilepsy, obsessive compulsive disorder). As the mind and body undergo the ageing process, co-existing conditions can change. New conditions may develop, some of which may be related to ageing, such as dementia, arthritis and osteoporosis and so on. Carers or family members who know the person well should be alert to any changes and the possible reasons for them. This may include looking at changes in physical health, such as weight, eyesight, hearing, mobility and breathing. Changes in mood or behaviour may also signal and underlying problem. Any changes noticed should always be discussed with a GP or other health professional.

However, it is also important not to make any assumptions about physical or cognitive decline changes on the basis of age alone and to have an open mind about possible causes.

Support and aids

As autistic people get older, they are likely to need more support, which could be through the help of carers or aids that can make daily tasks easier. There are many aids available now that can help with hearing, walking, sitting, turning taps on and off, reminding people to take medications and many more. Some people are starting to use assistive technology to retain their independence and promote their dignity, including apps on tablets. Not all these items will be specific to older adults with autism but a lot of them can be adapted or used in a more autism-specific way.

When a person's abilities start to decline, it is advisable to seek advice from a physiotherapist or occupational therapist to make sure that the correct equipment to meet their needs is chosen. Referrals can be made through GP's and social services departments.

Death and bereavement

Planning for death

Calderstones Partnership NHS Foundation Trust created a document called a *Plan for When I Die* that NAS adapted for people on the autism spectrum. This plan looks at everything that needs to be considered and the decisions that will have to be made after a person with autism has died. Talking about funeral arrangements and where possessions will go can be difficult, but giving a person the chance to think about this and share their views and wishes is important. These include:

- whether the person wants to be buried or cremated
- what sort of funeral they would like
- whether they would like any specific songs played
- whether they would like a religious figure to be present
- where and to whom their personal possessions should go.

Dealing with the death of someone close to you

People with autism (including Asperger syndrome) need support following the death of someone close to them, just like anyone else. If someone uses a service, a bereavement questionnaire can help staff to provide that support. The NAS services has developed a useful questionnaire which may help caregivers following a bereavement. The questionnaire looks at:

- support during bereavement
- financial and legal arrangements
- supportive relationships
- parents' and carers' wishes
- views about death.

The NAS also covers a range of useful topics including:

- housing options for older people
- social security benefits for older people
- social isolation
- dental care and autism
- managing money
- age-related conditions.

References

Barber C (2015) Old age and people on the autism spectrum: a focus group perspective. *British Journal of Nursing* **24** (21).

Bennett M (2016) "What is life like in the twilight years?" A letter about the scant amount of literature on the elderly with autism spectrum disorders. *Journal of Autism and Developmental Disorders* **46** (5) 1883–1884.

Bibby R (2012) 'I hope he goes first': exploring determinants of engagement in future planning for adults with a learning disability living with ageing parents. What are the issues? A literature review. *British Journal of Learning Disabilities* **41** 94–105.

Blackman N (2007) People with learning disabilities – an ageing population. *The Journal of Adult Protection* **9** (3) 3–8.

D'Astous V, Manthorpe J, Lowton K & Glaser K (2014) Retracing the historical social care context of autism: a narrative overview. *The British Journal of Social Work* **46** (3) 789–807.

Dunn Y The impact of the Care Act 2014 for autistic adults with an intellectual disability in England. In: D Milton and N Martin (Eds) *Autism and Intellectual disability in Adults, Volume 1.* Brighton: Pavilion Publishing & Media pp19-25.

Glover G, Emerson E & Evison F (2013) The uptake of health checks for adults with learning disabilities in England: 2008/9-2011/12. *Tizard Learning Disability Review* **18** (1) 45–49.

Harbottle C & Jones M (2016) Total attachment. A whole systems approach to safeguarding adults in care services. In: D Milton and N Martin (Eds) *Autism and Intellectual disability in Adults, Volume 1.* Brighton: Pavilion Publishing & Media.

Heslop P, Blair PS, Fleming PJ, Hoghton MA, Marriott AM & Russ LS (2013) *Confidential Inquiry into Premature Deaths of People with Learning Disabilities (CIPOLD): Final report.* Norah Fry Research Centre.

Lever AG & Geurts HM (2016) Psychiatric co-occurring symptoms and disorders in young, middle-aged, and older adults with autism spectrum disorder. *Journal of Autism and Developmental Disorders*, **46**(6),1916–1930.

McCarthy M & Millard L (2003) Discussing the menopause with women with learning difficulties. *British Journal of Learning Disabilities* **31** 9–17.

McPartland JC, Law K & Dawson G (2015) Autism spectrum disorder. In: H Friedman (Ed.) *Encyclopedia of Mental Health (2nd edition)* (pp124–130). London: Elsevier.

Michael C (2016) Why we need research about autism and ageing. *Autism* **20** (5) 515–516.

Milton D & Sims T (2016) How is a sense of well-being and belonging constructed in the accounts of autistic adults? *Disability & Society* **31** (4) 520–534.

NHS England & Age UK (2015) *A Practical Guide to Healthy Ageing* [online]. Available at: https://www.england.nhs.uk/wp-content/uploads/2015/09/hlthy-ageing-brochr.pdf (accessed September 2017)

Piven J & Rabins P (2011) Autism spectrum disorders in older adults: toward defining a research agenda. *Journal of the American Geriatrics Society* **59** (11) 2151–2155.

Public Health England (2014) *Making Reasonable Adjustments to End of Life Care for People with Learning Disabilities* [online]. Available at: https://www.ndti.org.uk/uploads/files/RA-End_of_Life.pdf (accessed September 2017)

Totsika V, Felce D, Kerr M & Hastings RP (2010) Behavior problems, psychiatric symptoms, and quality of life for older adults with intellectual disability with and without autism. *Journal of Autism and Developmental Disorders*, **40**(10) 1171–1178.

Walker C & Ward C (2013) Growing older together: ageing and people with learning disabilities and their family carers. *Tizard Learning Disability Review* **18** (3) 112–119.

Wallace GL, Budgett J & Charlton RA (2016) Aging and autism spectrum disorder: Evidence from the broad autism phenotype. *Autism Research* **9** (12) 1294–1303.

Additional resources

http://www.autism.org.uk/about/adult-life/ageing.aspx

http://www.autism.org.uk/about/adult-life/ageing/aim-project.aspx

NAS resources

Ageing With Autism - A handbook for care and support professionals

An in-depth guide for professionals who work with older autistic people every day. It looks at a number of issues that older people are likely to face, including physical or mental health problems; change; transition; and bereavement. It suggests ways in which these issues might be managed, with a focus on the older person's quality of life.

Ageing with Autism: A guide for clinicians and health professionals

An at-a-glance e-book guide to some of the main issues faced by older autistic people. It is aimed at professionals such as GPs and hospital staff who may come into contact with autistic people from time-to-time.

Useful resources from Pavilion

Hall of Mirrors – Shards of Clarity:
Autism, neuroscience and finding a sense of self

by Phoebe Caldwell

Drawing on Phoebe Caldwell's 40 years of experience and expert knowledge of autism and Intensive Interaction, *Hall of Mirrors – Shards of Clarity* marries recent neuroscience research evidence and practical approaches used in care to cover a wide range of vital subjects. Sense of self, confirmation, sensory issues, case studies and neuroscience findings are explored and weaved together in an inspired way which brings aims to bring theory into practice and vice versa, while at the same time listening to the voices of people with autism. The result is to allow everyone in the autism field to take a few steps forward with how they interact and support autistic people.

Available at: https://www.pavpub.com/hall-of-mirrors/

A Mismatch of Salience:
Explorations of the nature of autism from theory to practice

by Damian Milton

A Mismatch of Salience brings together a range of Damian Milton's writings that span more than a decade. The book explores the communication and understanding difficulties that can create barriers between people on the autism spectrum and neurotypical people. It celebrates diversity in communication styles and human experience by re framing the view that autistic people represent a 'disordered other' not as an impairment, but a two-way mismatch of salience. It also looks at how our current knowledge has been created by non-autistic people on the 'outside', looking in. *A Mismatch of Salience* attempts to redress this balance.

Available at: https://www.pavpub.com/a-mismatch-of-salience/

10 Rules for Ensuring People with Learning Disabilities and those who are on the Autism Spectrum Develop 'Challenging Behaviour' …And maybe what we can do about it

by Damian Milton, Richard Mills and Simon Jones

Written in the voice of someone with autism, this pocket sized booklet directly addresses the many practices and assumptions that that cause so many problems for children and adults with autism and learning difficulties and their family, friends and carers.

Available at: https://www.pavpub.com/10-rules-for-challenging-behaviour/

The Anger Box:
Sensory turmoil and pain in autism

by Phoebe Caldwell

In this book the author draws upon her wealth of experience to explore and attempt to understand the sensory issues, and their neurobiological roots, experienced by those on the autistic spectrum in an effort to find new ways of alleviating the distress that can characterise adults and children on the autistic spectrum.

Available at: https://www.pavpub.com/the-anger-box/

Understanding Autism:
A training pack for support staff and professionals based on 'Postcards from Aspie World'

by Dan Redfearn, Holly Turton, Helen Larder and Hayden Larder

This unique training pack is based on the premise that learning from the experience of someone on the autism spectrum can help those who support individuals to understand and to adapt their approach and therefore achieve better outcomes. Each pack comes with a set of postcards created by a young woman with Asperger's syndrome. The postcards are also available to buy separately and are a valuable resource to prompt and aid discussion.

Available at: https://www.pavpub.com/understanding-autism/

Choosing Autism Interventions:
A research-based guide

by Bernard Fleming, Elisabeth Hurley and The Goth

This best-selling book provides an accessible evidence-based overview of the most commonly used interventions for children and adults on the autism spectrum. It summarises best clinical practice from the National Institute for Health and Care Excellence (NICE) and gives a set of tools to help you evaluate interventions for yourself. It is the first guide of its kind to meet the requirements of the NHS Information Standard.

Available at: https://www.pavpub.com/choosing-autism-interventions/

Autism Spectrum Conditions:
A guide

by Eddie Chaplin, Steve Hardy and Lisa Underwood

Published in association with the Estia Centre, this guide provides a comprehensive introduction to working with people who have autism spectrum conditions.

Available at: https://www.pavpub.com/autism-spectrum-conditions/

Delicious Conversations:
Reflections on autism, intimacy and communication

by Phoebe Caldwell

Through her compelling reflections Caldwell shows us that by tuning in to our partners' body language we can not only communicate with people with autism but also share an emotional connection, helping to combat the isolating nature of autistic spectrum conditions.

Available at: https://www.pavpub.com/delicious-conversations/

Understanding and Supporting Children and Adults on the Autism Spectrum

by Julie Beadle-Brown and Richard Mills

This unique multi-media training and learning resource, informed by both research and practice, is written by experts and designed not only to help people understand autism spectrum conditions but also to give them a person-centred framework of intervention and support for children or adults on the autism spectrum.

Available at: https://www.pavpub.com/understanding-and-supporting-children-andadults-on-the-autism-spectrum/

Autism Arts Levels 1, 2 & 3

by Abigail Barragry

Autism Arts is a drama syllabus that encourages children who are on the autism spectrum to express themselves, interact and use their imaginations.

Available at: https://www.pavpub.com/autism-arts-level-1/

Notes